BEFORE DEPORTATION

Letters from a Mother to Her Daughters
January 1939–December 1942

HERTHA FEINER

Edited and with an Introduction by Karl Heinz Jahnke
Translated from the German by Margot Bettauer Dembo

NORTHWESTERN UNIVERSITY PRESS
Evanston, Illinois

Northwestern University Press
Evanston, Illinois 60208-4210

Originally published in German under the title *Von der Deportation*. Copyright
© 1993 Fischer Taschenbuch Verlag GmbH, Frankfurt am Main. English trans-
lation copyright © 1999 by Northwestern University Press. Published 1999.
All rights reserved.

Printed in the United States of America

ISBN 0-8101-1474-7 (cloth)
ISBN 0-8101-1475-5 (paper)

Library of Congress Cataloging-in-Publication Data

Feiner, Hertha, 1896–1943.
  [Von der Deportation.   English]
  Before deportation : letters from a mother to her daughters,
January 1939–December 1942 / Hertha Feiner ; edited with
introduction by Karl Heinz Jahnke ; translated from the German by
Margot Bettauer Dembo.
      p.   cm.
  ISBN 0-8101-1474-7 (cloth). — ISBN 0-8101-1475-5 (paper)
  1. Feiner, Hertha, 1896–1943—Correspondence. 2. Jews—Germany—
Correspondence. 3. Jews—Germany—History—1933–1945.
4. Holocaust, Jewish (1939–1945). I. Jahnke, Karl Heinz.
II. Title.
DS135.G5F36413   1999
940.53'18'092—dc21
[B]   99-12406
                                                          CIP

The paper used in this publication meets the minimum requirements of the
American National Standard for Information Sciences—
Permanence of Paper for Printed Library Materials, ANSI
Z39.48-1984.

*Translator's Note: Explanatory material appearing within brackets has been
provided by the translator.*

Before Deportation

✿

Contents

❀

Acknowledgments

There has been no previous mention of Hertha Feiner in Holocaust literature. I first heard about this admirable woman in 1957 from her daughter Inge Flehmig. For a long time I searched for some reliable sources from which to re-create a picture of her life. But in vain.

After the collapse of the GDR in 1989, there were suddenly new opportunities to get more material. Pupils of the Meerweinstrasse School in Hamburg, where Hertha Feiner had taught, had gathered information about her, and this was a help. Due to their perseverance, Inge Flehmig eventually saw the documents that had been preserved. Subsequently, Dr. Flehmig made available more than eighty letters that Hertha Feiner had written to Gland, Switzerland, between 1939 and 1942. Hertha's other daughter, Marion Boyars, provided additional letters, so that altogether 124 letters became available. Fifty-seven of them are included in this volume.

I was able to obtain supplementary information about the deportation of Berlin's Jews in the years 1941 to 1943 from the files of the Berlin State Archives (Landesarchiv Berlin). In my research I did not come across Heinz Landau's name after 1945. It is probably that Landau, who had stayed on in Berlin for Hertha's sake, was deported to Auschwitz on a later transport.

Without the help of friends and colleagues, as well as the assistance of people who had known Hertha Feiner, I could not have completed this book.

Therefore, I especially thank Marion Boyars, Dr. Inge Flehmig, Dr. Rolf Flehmig, Renate Friederichs, Roland

Gröschel, Heidi Jahnke, Frank Leimkugel, Rita Meyhöfer, Georg von Prosch, Ursula Randt, Ulla Rühl, and Günter Wehner.

Karl Heinz Jahnke
Rostock
October 1992

❧

Introduction

This book contains some of the letters Hertha Feiner wrote from Berlin to her daughters, Marion and Inge, between January 29, 1939, and December 17, 1942.

After the horror of Kristallnacht, the pogrom against the Jews in November 1938, Hertha agreed with her husband's suggestion that their daughters be sent to a Swiss boarding school in Gland on Lake Geneva. The girls were eleven and fourteen when they left Berlin at the end of January 1939.

Until November 1941, Hertha was able to work as a teacher in the Jewish school on Fasanenstrasse 79–80 in Charlottenburg and later on Auguststrasse 11–17. After her dismissal as a teacher, she worked for the Jewish Community, helping with preparations for the deportation of tens of thousands of Jews from Berlin. In March 1943, she herself was sent to the Auschwitz death camp.

Her letters are a unique testimony to that time. In addition to many personal details, they also contain specifics about what was happening in Berlin's Jewish schools and the everyday life of a Jewish woman living in the city under National Socialist rule.

Hertha's father, Joseph Feiner, had been appointed by the Jewish Communities to teach in Sonsbeck on the lower Rhine (Niederrhein) in 1884 and then in Finsterwalde after 1889. From 1892 on, he taught in Hamburg at the Anton Ree School and was principal there for several years. In addition, he served for many years on the Repräsentanten-Kollegium of the Hamburg Jewish Community. Hertha's mother, Fanny

Feiner, whose maiden name was Fröhlich, came from a well-to-do family of businesspeople in the Rhine region. Joseph and Fanny Feiner had three children: Hermann, the oldest; Hertha, who was born two years later on May 8, 1896; and Erich, who was three years younger than his sister. Fanny Feiner died in 1917.

Encouraged by her father, Hertha decided to become a teacher. After graduating from high school, she enrolled at Hamburg University to study pedagogy. She landed her first position in 1923 as teacher and tutor at a boarding school in Bad Harzburg. In later years, she looked back on this period as one of the happiest of her life. In 1924, she returned to Hamburg, her hometown, where she held several teaching positions, one of them at the Meerweinstrasse school in Barmbek. That same year, she married Johannes Asmus, a publisher and bookseller. Her family did not approve of this marriage to a non-Jew.

A daughter, Inge, was born to Hertha and Johannes on January 24, 1925, and two and a half years later, on October 26, 1927, the second child, Marion, was born. The marriage was not a happy one. Evidently, the couple's personalities and interests were incompatible. An added complication came from their precarious financial situation. As a publisher, Johannes had difficulty providing for the material needs of his family, and Hertha's salary as a teacher was meager at that time. Things became especially rocky when, because of the national economic crisis, Johannes had to declare bankruptcy.

In spite of these constant worries, Hertha tried to provide a carefree atmosphere for her children. She devoted much of her time to them, and her joyful and optimistic nature had a distinct effect on her daughters.

Early in 1933, Hertha and Johannes were divorced. Hertha was awarded custody of the children and assumed her maiden name.

In April 1933, when the National Socialists came to power, Hertha was dismissed from her teaching job because she was Jewish. She was out of work for several months. But then, with help from her father and the Jewish Community in

Hamburg, she obtained a position as an assistant teacher in the Jewish school on Johnsallee and managed to support her little family on her scanty wages.

Because the situation was difficult in Hamburg, Hertha looked for a chance to go elsewhere to start over. The opportunity came in April 1935 when she was offered a teaching position at a private Jewish school in Berlin, the Waldschule in the Grunewald section of Berlin (Hagenstrasse 56), also called the Lessler School after the two sisters who had founded it and were running it. Hertha worked there enthusiastically until the middle of 1938. Inge was a student at this school. But it became increasingly difficult to keep the school going, and Hertha transferred to a teaching job at the Jewish public school at 79–80 Fasanenstrasse, in the center of Berlin's Jewish Community.

During those first years in Berlin, Hertha and her daughters lived on the edge of poverty. They sublet one room from a man named Engelhardt who had a grocery store on Rheinbabenallee. Then in 1936, they were able to rent a three-room apartment at 104 Rudolstädter Strasse in the Wilmersdorf section of Berlin.

From those of Hertha's writings that have survived, it appears that she considered the years between 1935 and the fall of 1938 a joyful time. She steadfastly tried to keep her children from finding out about the hostility and growing brutality shown toward Jews and dissidents. Apparently, she had illusions about the future of Germany and refused to accept the reality of much of what was happening around her, trying to suppress anything unpleasant.

The financial situation of the family was somewhat better than it had been in Hamburg. Hertha could afford a roomy apartment and household help. On weekends and during vacations, she and her daughters went on excursions into the surrounding countryside and even beyond. For instance, in 1937 they went to the Riesengebirge, the Giant Mountains. Hertha tried to create a small, safe world for herself and her children even though the hostile and inhuman measures directed toward the Jews by the Nazis gradually began to encroach on their lives.

Her father and her older brother Hermann had committed suicide in 1936 because they could no longer face the constant anti-Jewish harassment. In 1934 the name of Joseph Feiner, who had been a highly respected pedagogue, was removed from all Hamburg directories. Hermann had been relieved of his position as a judge in the Hamburg State Court soon after the Nazis came to power.

From 1938 on, more and more of the Feiners' friends and relatives, the families of Hertha's students, and her daughters' classmates left Germany. Among those who emigrated was Hertha's younger brother Erich. After Kristallnacht on November 9, Hertha began to realize that her children would have to leave Germany as quickly as possible.

Johannes Asmus, their father, made the necessary arrangements, working through his connections with publishers in Switzerland. At the end of January 1939, Inge and Marion left Berlin for Switzerland. They were headed for Les Rayons, a school founded by Dr. Max Bondy in Gland on Lake Geneva (Canton Waadt). Between thirty and forty boys and girls, most of them from Jewish or "half-Jewish" families, lived at this boarding school. The staff also acted as teachers. In Gland the Feiner girls received a classical education and were able to grow up largely unaffected by the turbulence of the times.

The letters Hertha exchanged regularly with her daughters were the most important link between them. In 1939 and until early 1940, it was also still possible to stay in touch by telephone. The first letter the girls received from their mother was dated January 29, 1939. Like many of her later letters, it reveals how worried she is about her children. How would they—on their own for the first time and in a strange country—be able to adjust, to feel at home? Would they have the necessary strength and understanding to take advantage of the opportunity offered by the school to get a thorough education? And would the girls, so different from each other, get along?

Hertha constantly tried to give her children advice as both a mother and friend; she sent the girls books to read and tried to initiate discussions about what they were reading. In her own way, she did everything possible to keep the bond between her daughters and herself intact. And so they sent each other detailed reports about their experiences in Berlin and in Gland.

Hertha energetically pursued her career as a teacher. On June 4, 1939, she wrote to her daughters: "As I get to know them better, I'm getting to like the children in school more and more" [letter does not appear in this book]. At the same time, she was sad that so many of her friends and acquaintances were leaving Germany. By August 8, only fourteen children of the thirty-five who had started the new school year in April were left. Many of the young teachers who had become her friends had emigrated. She was depressed by the fact that all her own efforts to find a way to get out of Germany had proved unsuccessful.

The financial resources of the Jewish Community, which had been bearing full responsibility for running the Jewish schools since the end of 1938, were quite limited. Consequently, teachers were paid very little. On several occasions, Hertha mentions that she was not paid on time. To earn additional money, she gave private English lessons to adults preparing to emigrate. After her daughters left, she sold some of her furniture and rented out two of the rooms in her apartment, one to Max and Anna Marcus, a Jewish teacher and his non-Jewish wife, and the other to a Miss Meyer, also a teacher at one of the Jewish schools. In the spring of 1939, when many Jews were forced to give up their apartments, Hertha was able to continue living on Rudolstädter Strasse because the Nazi decree of December 28, 1938, permitted a family to remain in their apartment if the father was Aryan and the mother Jewish.

So the situation under the Nazis was somewhat better for Hertha than for many other Jewish residents. She could stay in her own apartment and continue working as a teacher. She was also able to get away for vacations, staying in Jewish boardinghouses or hotels. During her Easter vacation in 1939, she spent a few days at the Semmering in the foothills of the Alps in eastern Austria. Then in early August, she went to

Friedrichroda, a town in the Thuringian Forest of eastern Germany, for a week.

The nicest thing that happened during these first difficult months of separation must surely have been that Inge and Marion were able to visit her in July 1939. They were together for three happy weeks, and Hertha took more time to be with her children than she had ever done before. Their parting at the end of July would turn out to be the last time they saw one another.

The beginning of the Second World War on September 1, 1939, had drastic consequences for Hertha and her daughters. Yet at first the letters reflect that in only a limited way. On August 30, Hertha wrote: "Last Saturday I bought a dress for school and a smock; one needs a ration card for this now." Otherwise, almost everything seemed to be as it had been before. But her letter of September 4 reports that the Jewish schools in Berlin had remained closed during the first days of the war. She seems deeply worried that she would not be able to keep up the correspondence with her daughters.

Her October letters indicate that significant changes had taken place: "All in all, a lot has changed since you left. I haven't been out a single evening since September 1; all our people are home by 8:00 P.M." [letter does not appear in this book]. This was the result of a curfew imposed by the police at the beginning of the war ordering Jews to be inside their apartments by 9:00 P.M. in the summer and by 8:00 P.M. in the winter. The curtailment of the activities of the Jewish Kulturbund, the Jewish Cultural Association, saddened Hertha and her friends: "The only thing the Kulturbund still offers is movies; there is no more theater" [letter does not appear in this book].

With dismay, Hertha watched the dismissal of many teachers who were her friends. On the other hand, she was glad that she herself was permitted to continue her teaching. In a letter dated November 26, 1939, she describes a Hanukkah celebration her class presented; it gives us a hint of her relationship with her pupils and what her work as teacher entailed: "[W]e thought of something on our own: Some children want to celebrate Hanukkah using their dolls. They improvise quite freely. A poor man comes along and they give him all the food they have. But then their mother gives them more food. We intersperse this with German and Hebrew poems and songs. One of the children sings in Turkish, another in Polish, a third in French."

Hertha spent Christmas of 1939 and the 1940 New Year holidays taking a refresher course for English teachers offered by the Reichsvereinigung der Juden [Reich Organization of Jews] in the School of Horticulture near Hanover.

The weeks that followed her return to Berlin were miserable. The frigid weather and the meager financial resources of the Jewish Community meant that practically no classes were held at Hertha's school from January to March 1940. Her letters to Marion and Inge make mention of this. For instance, in a letter in early February, she writes: "It is bitterly cold here — -20° C [-4° F]. There's no school; we meet only on Wednesdays in the unheated classrooms to check the homework assignments and to hand out new ones." In March she writes: "The [real] vacation starts on March 20; I don't think we will be working from now till then. But we have to make out report cards, and some children have to be left back. We've hardly had any school since January."

In the spring of 1940, Hertha finally realized that she must leave Germany. She registered at the American consulate to obtain an immigrant visa for the United States and asked Inge to persuade relatives to help her. On June 2 she wrote to Inge: "My registration number is very high; I applied too late. I am number 77,454 under the German quota, which means I will have to wait at least five to six years" [letter does not appear in this book].

As living conditions for Jews in Germany steadily deteriorated, Hertha became more determined than ever to leave. She felt a growing sense of emptiness and loneliness as more and more of her acquaintances and friends left in the first half of 1940. A sentence in her letter of March 27 hints at this: "Soon there'll be only old people left here."

Yet in spite of all her efforts, there seemed to be no feasible way for her to get out of Germany. Hertha was profoundly depressed by this, but she tried to keep it from her daughters.

One can imagine how painful the intensified restrictions were that the Nazis imposed on all forms of communication by Jews, both within the country and abroad. On October 1, 1940, the Reich postal minister decreed that Jews would no longer be permitted to have telephones. Fortunately for Hertha, that was not as bad as it might have been because her lodger Anna Marcus, who was not Jewish, was able to obtain a phone. Mail going abroad was also severely curtailed. Letters had to be written in German and could not exceed four pages in length. There were repeated admonitions not to send letters too frequently. (For each letter that was mailed, one received only a single coupon entitling the addressee to send a letter in reply.)

After the 1940 summer vacation, the situation at Hertha's school became even worse. The school had to move out of the building it had been using. More teachers were fired, and all classes of the same grade level were combined. Hertha reports on these developments in a letter dated October 16: "But first I want to tell you that we are no longer in our beautiful school building. Yesterday we moved into an old house, but we already have to move out of there, too. Yes, indeed—no comment needed. Now we don't know where we will be teaching, and there are forty-six children in my class."

Of inestimable value to Hertha—besides the exchange of letters with her daughters—were the contacts she had with other people, and their concern and offers of help. Evidently the Jewish teachers in Berlin stuck together as a group. In addition, Hertha maintained contacts with many of her students' parents and with former students. She enjoyed getting together with the young people who lived with her daughters in Switzerland whenever any of them came to Berlin. In this way she received direct news and reassurance about her children and made new friends. Some of these visitors were the children of families that were part Jewish, and others of families that were not Jewish.

In the fall of 1940, Hertha met Heinz Landau in an English

class she was attending to prepare for emigration. He was a pharmacist and had been the manager of the Concordia Pharmacy at 70 Kastanienallee in Berlin. The anti-Semitic policies of the Nazi regime had deprived him of practicing his profession, and he was now taking intensive English courses in preparation for his departure for the United States, where his sister lived.

From that time on, Heinz and Hertha met often. They helped each other, and a close relationship developed as they prepared for their departure. Both still hoped to emigrate to America.

In January 1941, Hertha began taking a course in hat making. She felt that this specialty would make it possible to earn a living for herself and her daughters in America. On March 11, she wrote to Inge that the situation in Berlin was becoming worse: "We are going through troubled times here so that, in spite of my great longing for you, I am glad you are spared this and can work in peace. I wrote to Marion yesterday that many teachers have been fired: of 230 teachers, only 100 remain, and since quite a few of them are tenured (that is, they have been with the [Jewish] Community since before 1928) and cannot be dismissed, you can imagine how bleak my prospects are. A decision is expected by April 1. Mssrs. Marcus, Birnbaum, Misch, and Neufeld have already been let go, and now they are assigned by the Community to finding apartments for young people who don't have any."

On March 31, after several weeks of uncertainty, Hertha was able to write: "For the time being, I am staying on at the school. About 100 teachers were let go, others were transferred, but nothing happened to me, thank God. The only thing is that now, in the new semester, I have to teach a lot of physical education [classes] because no one else can do it" [letter does not appear in this book]. That year, instead of getting an Easter vacation, the teachers had to work for the Jewish Community.

An edict effective immediately was issued on April 26, 1941, in Berlin by the Reich minister for education and instruction of the Reichsvereinigung der Juden. It called for the further dismantling of the Jewish school system. Hertha's letter reported that another forty-two teachers were dismissed. On June 1, while she was working at the girls' school on Auguststrasse, she wrote: "Work at school is very strenuous now. Because of the dismissal of so many teachers, we work longer hours while at the same time our salaries have been cut. But the Community is not doing well [financially], and there's nothing that can be done about it. The many hours of teaching physical education (24 hours a week) are very tiring."

The letters to her daughters also contain information about the daily life of Jews in Berlin, such as descriptions of the working conditions and living conditions of forced laborers in industry and agriculture. For instance, one of the former teachers had been assigned to a textile factory. Hertha writes about her on July 31: "One of my colleagues who was fired has to sew linings into children's coats and is paid 30 pfennig apiece (she works an hour on each coat), and she has to live on that" [letter does not appear in this book].

On July 14 she wrote to Inge about Jews being chased out of their apartments: "Yes—a very depressed Uncle Alfred wrote me that many people are now living in his apartment. Thank God, I can stay in mine. You probably can't imagine what this means. So many moving vans were parked on our street today" [letter does not appear in this book]. Hertha was permitted to stay in her apartment because her two daughters were counted as part of her household.

Many of the letters she wrote to Gland indicate what an important role discussions about books played for her during these difficult times; she mentions Goethe, Voltaire, Nietzsche, Schopenhauer, and Wiechert. Various entertainments staged at the Jewish Kulturbund provided a change of pace and an atmosphere of relaxation, although the organization was increasingly hampered in its activities. On June 17, for instance, Hertha wrote to her daughters: "Saturday evening I went to our theater and it was really quite nice. There was music by Offenbach and a witty, clever piece called *Senor Alan aus dem Fegefeuer* [*Señor Alan Arrives from Pur-*

gatory, by S. López]. It was so entertaining that for two hours we forgot all our troubles" [letter does not appear in this book].

The few details the letters contain about the war and its effects, and the air raids on Berlin, are hidden in ambiguous phrases. An example is this excerpt from a letter sent on September 7: "I have to go to school now. Last night we slept very little, and school starts at 10 o'clock, and the children are very restless."

On October 16, 1941, Hertha wrote to her children: "We have serious worries and are living through a very grave time. I can't and won't burden you with details; I'm fortunate in being better off than many others. You don't have to worry about me. Because of my special status I hope to be able to go on living here as before."

By "special status" she meant that, because she had been married to a non-Jew and had two daughters from this marriage, she was allowed to stay in her apartment. She also believed that she would not be deported.

October 18 marked the start of the deportation of Berlin's Jews to concentration camps, where they were to be murdered. The Nazi regime had definitively switched to its policy of exterminating the Jews. This also included the seizure and confiscation of all Jewish property, as well as a prohibition on any further emigration, in accordance with a decree issued on October 23. At this point it became apparent that at least one of her daughters, if not both, had to return to Berlin to live with her as a form of protection. She tried to convince her former husband, who was now living in Leipzig, to help with this move. He had been paying Inge and Marion's tuition and other expenses in Switzerland and was also in direct contact with them.

Hertha's relationship with her ex-husband, which had been quite cool before, now underwent further distressing changes. One important reason for this probably was that Johannes Asmus had remarried. His wife, Hermine, an ardent Nazi, had divorced her previous husband because he was Jewish.

At first, Hertha expected Johannes and Hermine to help

her to stay in touch with her daughters under the increasingly difficult conditions and, if necessary, to come up with a solution that would save her life. But just the opposite happened. Contact with her daughters became less frequent because of pressure exerted on them from Leipzig. Asmus suggested to the girls that they write to their mother less often. And yet in these hard and trying weeks, Hertha desperately needed to keep in touch with her daughters. On October 23, 1941, she wrote to Inge: "Why do you write so seldom? In these hard times, your letters are more important to me than bread. I am terribly sorry that I couldn't send a happier letter to Marion for her birthday, but I feel so very sad—not at all like the person you used to know—and at the moment I can't imagine a time when things will ever be all right again." These words were written after the arrest of Heinz Landau, her closest friend. Apparently he was one of the first Jews to be assigned for deportation in October.

On November 2, Hertha wrote that she was "in a somewhat better mood today because a miracle has happened. Heinz L. was gone and has come back." On November 5, she added: "At the moment I feel somewhat better because I'm not alone. Both of us [Heinz and I] still think it was a miracle. We don't know how long this miracle will last, but we've long ago rid ourselves of the habit of thinking beyond the next day." To this day, no one knows why Heinz Landau was released.

In November 1941, additional restrictions were imposed on the Jewish school system. This time around, Hertha was among the many teachers who were dismissed. On November 25, she wrote her daughters about this, in words full of pain and sorrow: "I am sad not to be with my schoolchildren anymore, even more so because they now have a teacher who is over sixty and does not like teaching. I didn't even say good-bye to the children, since I was dismissed on Sunday and my new work began on Monday at 7:00 A.M."

At first Hertha was assigned to the land registry office of the Jewish Community. Her job was to register all Jews residing in Berlin [about 70,000 people]. This new and unfamiliar work taxed her strength. In a New Year's letter written on December 29, 1941, she took stock: "I've gotten used to my new work and resigned myself to my fate—if only things don't get worse."

Foremost among her hopes for the new year is "Peace, that is our most heartfelt wish, so that all those who are far away and who are suffering so much can return home. I have one great desire: that we three shall be reunited."

The year 1942 was to be the hardest year of her life. As an employee of the Berlin Jewish Community, she experienced directly the brutality of the Nazi rulers. Since one of her duties was to help in the preparation of deportation lists, she was one of the last in the Jewish Community to have contact with those who had to report for the numerous transports to death in the concentration camps. In her letters there is a clear picture of the horrors she faced daily. Many of her friends, acquaintances, and quite a few of her former pupils were among those selected for deportation. On January 13, Walter Matzdorff, a man she knew well, was put on a transport to Riga. On January 11 she wrote to her children: "We are going through a very grave period here. This time Walter Matzdorff and many of my pupils are on the list [for deportation]. I have to work hard and try to help as many people as possible."

Shortly before Easter, on April 2, Hertha apologized for not having written as often as before: "I feel quite guilty for not having written for such a long time, but I have to do a great deal of work that is very unpleasant. . . . Help me in these difficult times and write to me often and in detail (even if I don't always answer promptly) because your letters and my thoughts of you are the only rays of hope I have."

To give her children some insight into conditions in Berlin, she also wrote about people she knew who were now forced laborers in the armaments industry. For instance, on January 16, she reports on a former classmate of Inge's: "Take Gisela Michaelis, for instance; she is one of Aunt Irma's coworkers now and has to leave the house at 5:00 A.M.; she has to do the same dull, tedious work all day long. And when she comes home in the evening, she is content to simply go to bed."

On March 18 she tells her children about Max Marcus, the Jewish teacher who lives with his Aryan wife in her apartment: "Mr. Marcus is having a difficult time. He works in a factory as a laborer; this week his hours are from 6:00 in the evening to 6:00 in the morning (when I take the bus into the city, he is just coming home), and last week he had to get up at 4:00 in the morning to go to work. His wife helps him valiantly and tries to make things as easy for him as she possibly can."

In spite of her difficult everyday life, Hertha never stopped trying to influence the development and education of her children. She gave them advice about which books to read and tried to keep up an exchange of opinions about what they had read. She was very much aware how decisive these years in the lives of her fourteen- and seventeen-year-old girls were in the development of their character. She was especially concerned with Inge's vocational education.

It must have been particularly difficult for Hertha to be separated from her children when they informed her that they were joining the Protestant Church and would be baptized. In a letter to Marion dated April 5, Hertha discusses their intention in detail and describes her relationship to her children:

"Marion, you're right in saying that I brought you up so you would become familiar with everything and then make your own choices some day. . . . You must, however, be aware that one can't change one's faith like a shirt. Rather, when you say, 'I am going to profess my faith in the Christian religion,' then you have to stick to it. . . . I was born a Jew and would never have committed myself to another religion. You two have a choice, and I will not stand in the way of your doing whatever you want to do, so long as your decision is true and genuine and not made just because you are being swayed momentarily. Search your hearts long and hard, and then choose!"

In many of her letters, Hertha indicates how glad she is that her daughters are able to live in peace in Switzerland and get a proper education. Up to this point she had, for the most part, avoided burdening her children with descriptions of the many humiliations, the terror, and the misery Jewish citizens were experiencing in Nazi Germany. Because her children were "half-Jews," she benefited from certain "considerations" the Nazis accorded her.

At the beginning of the summer of 1942, however, it became clear that she had but one desperate chance to avoid deportation and death—one, if not both, of her children would have to come back to Berlin to live with her. On June 2, she asked that either Inge or Marion return to Berlin immediately: "[T]his can no longer be avoided, and you must share in my difficult life."

During that time, she wrote several insistent letters to Gland. In the middle of June, she was informed by the administrator of the boarding school that her letters had not been passed along to her daughters. On June 19, she wrote unequivocally to Inge and Marion: "Things are very serious here, and there is just one way out for me, and that's through you, either one or both of you. . . . If you want to see me again, one of you has to come to stay with me, and as soon as possible. . . . [I]f we can't manage to see each other now, there is absolutely no hope for later."

In spite of her frank words, her daughters did not come back to Berlin. They were kept from returning by their father and his new wife and by the director of the boarding school in Gland, Harald Baruschke. Hertha had placed her trust in him and others, and now, on discovering what they had done, she was dismayed and profoundly disappointed. Still, she tried to stay in touch with her children, to prevent a break in the connection. And until December 1942, in part through circuitous channels, she was able to continue the exchange of letters. Her letters document how the situation of Berlin's Jews was becoming steadily more hopeless.

"Things are going fairly well with me, but we have a lot of problems here. Miss Meyer is very sad just now and we are, too, because on Wednesday her mother is leaving" (July 12).

"I have many serious problems. Our circle of friends is steadily getting smaller. Your former teacher, Mr. Neufeld, died; he committed suicide. In recent weeks he looked so terrible, you would scarcely have recognized him" (July 22).

"Miss Meyer is no longer here" (August 9 [letter does not appear in this book]).

"Miss Schwartze and her mother are no longer here" (September 4).

"Dr. and Mrs. Opfer will leave this week and will never again hear anything from Margot and little Eva" (September 28).

"The Opfers are gone—there was no miracle" (October 1 [letter does not appear in this book]).

All the individuals she mentions in her letters were close acquaintances and friends who had been selected for deportation. Miss Meyer had been living in Hertha's apartment since February 1939. Miss Johanna Schwartze was a friend who had come to Berlin from Hamburg with her mother, Julie Schwartze. They were on the September 5, 1942, transport to Riga. On October 3, Dr. Felix Opfer and his wife, Doris, were on a transport of elderly Jews headed for the Theresienstadt concentration camp. Hertha was on friendly terms with their daughter Margot and their granddaughter Eva, who was the same age as Inge.

On September 28, Hertha wrote to Inge: "There are only a few people with whom I still get together, because many have left us, and besides, I have little time and need a tremendous amount of rest in order to keep my spiritual equilibrium." It is easy to understand how sad she felt because she received so few letters from Switzerland. She did not know that various efforts were being made to completely disrupt her contact with her children. Harald Baruschke, for instance, told the girls that too many letters could hurt their mother. The Asmus family in Leipzig broke off contact with Hertha almost completely.

The last letter the daughters received was dated December 17, 1942. It looks forward to Christmas: "Christmas is coming, the celebration of love. Let's hope that peace will come and all people who love one another will be reunited." She gives an indication of her state of mind: "I'm doing only so-so; if only you were here. I would so much like to be able to laugh again with all my heart; our lives are very serious these days."

In that letter, Hertha also declares how important it is to her to "have someone with whom I can share all my burdens." She is referring to Heinz Landau. Together, they were trying to bear up under their hard lot and to help each other.

Toward the end of 1942 and in the first weeks of 1943, more of Hertha's good friends and acquaintances in Berlin were deported. In December, twenty-two-year-old Hanna Litten, who had been active in the theater of the Jewish Kulturbund, was deported. On January 29, 1943, the names of Elisabeth and Kurt Friedländer and Alfred, their seventeen-year-old son, were on the list for the twenty-seventh transport to the Auschwitz extermination camp. On March 1, it was the turn of eighteen-year-old Gisela Michaelis, Inge's former classmate and friend.

These deportations were the result of the Nazis' "Factory Action" of February 27, 1943. On that day, without any prior notice, thousands of Jews were arrested at their workplaces and assembled in collection camps. From there, transports took them to Auschwitz. Between March 1 and March 6, more than seven thousand of Berlin's Jews started out on this, their final journey.

Up to that point, Jews who worked for the Jewish Community and the Reichsvertretung and who carried a "yellow identification certificate" had been spared. On March 9, this exemption, too, was canceled, and most of these people were arrested at their workplaces or in their apartments and taken to the collection camps.

Hertha was on the list of those to be deported. Two policemen came to her apartment to pick her up but did not find her there. She had been warned by other residents in the apartment house. With her remaining possessions packed into one suitcase, Hertha had gone to her former workplace at the Jewish Community. She was taken into custody there and brought to the collection camp on Grosse Hamburger Strasse. Anna Marcus tried to obtain her release, saying Hertha had two "half-Jewish" daughters ages eighteen and fifteen to take care of. But this brave last-minute attempt to get the Nazis to free Hertha failed.

On March 12, 1943, Hertha Feiner, along with 945 other Berlin Jews, began the journey to Auschwitz on the thirty-sixth transport east. Knowing full well that this was the end, she committed suicide during the train trip, swallowing a capsule of potassium cyanide that Heinz Landau had given her in case there was no other way out. Thus ended the life of an extraordinary woman.

Karl Heinz Jahnke

Before Deportation

❧

1939
JANUARY 29–DECEMBER 27

Berlin/Wilmersdorf, January 29, 1939
Rudolstädterstr. 104

My dear, sweet children,[1]

I received your lovely letter from Frankfurt. Many thanks, but you didn't send me your address, so today I will write to Zurich in the hope that my letter will be forwarded to you. You really had a fine trip, didn't you, and I'm sure things will continue to go well for you. Your detailed reports give me a lot of pleasure and I look forward to them. Enjoy everything to the utmost, especially glorious Nature, which is much more important than all the things made by human hands, and better, too. And in Nature we are all considered equal, whether poor or rich, Jewish or Christian, and no one needs to feel ashamed. I wonder where you are while I am writing this. I won't tell you what I am thinking and feeling because I don't want to burden you with my problems. But you know that I am with you, heart and soul. Ask me anything, tell me everything; I want to know everything and will answer all your questions. I wonder what sort of impression the new country and the people you'll meet will make on you.

I'll send my next letter to you at school. But by then I hope that I will have heard from you again.

Uncle Hans and his wife ask me to give you regards. Yesterday I spent the entire day with them. Their home is very nice. Today I received a long letter from the Hochschilds in Baltimore. They think of us often. They are doing well. I am supposed to send them your address (Inge, they send congratulations on your birthday).

I wonder if you're going to telephone Monday evening.

3

Before you go to sleep at night, please give each other a good-night kiss from me—you know what I mean. I am so glad that you are together. I'm sure Vati[2] is taking good care of you. I wonder if you're behaving according to the way I brought you up. I'm sure you are! Dear Inge, don't be too sensitive, and Marion, don't be too stuck-up. My thoughts, even though they don't know where you are, are always with you. They need neither a passport nor a train ticket!

Many warm hugs and kisses. I love you very much.

Your Mutti[3]

Berlin/Wilm. February 7, 1939

My dearest darlings,

You'll probably find this letter waiting for you when you come back from the ski lodge. I'm sure you had a great time; I hope to get a full report from you soon. Were you careful? Did you have good weather? Write me about everything and please be honest, even if it isn't all to your liking. I have to have the feeling that you're telling me everything. You know what I mean! There's little new to report from here. I haven't heard anything yet, and I no longer believe that I'll still be able to go to England. Aunt Irma has been hired as a lady's companion in England, and she can even take her mother along. She's returning from Vienna on the 14th of February and will then get ready to emigrate. And so, bit by bit, Berlin is emptying out.

I'm supposed to give you regards; you'll probably be most pleased to hear they come from Mr. Klimke and the man at the ticket gate. I am collecting "stars" for you, and when I have ten I'll send them to you. Would you like to have any other books? Books, as well as merchandise samples of up to 100 grams, can be mailed without paying customs duty. For the weekend I'll send you some sweets. I bought myself a good coat at Arnold Müller today; too bad you can't see it. Did I already write you that I sold the bedroom furniture for 300 RM [Reichsmark] and the kitchen things for 30 RM? The teachers and students who will still be at the Lessler School at Easter time are going to be merged into the Holdheim School.

There's nothing new in school. Unfortunately Mr. Poeschke didn't get any foreign currency, so for the time being, he can't visit you.

Vati wrote that he is coming to see me next week. By then I hope to have a clearer picture of things. Schnackchen sends you regards; she's already gone to bed.[4] She's certainly not suffering from overwork at the moment, as you can imagine. I still haven't sublet the rooms, but I'd like to find somebody nice to share the apartment.

Please write frankly about everything you think and do. I haven't yet written to the school. Let me know to whom I should address my letter; who is most trustworthy. Warmest wishes, hugs, and cuddling (in my thoughts you're both sitting on my lap). I love you sooo very much.

Your Mutti

Berlin, February 19, 1939

My dearest ones,

Sundays are ever so much nicer when a lovely letter from you drops through the mail slot in the morning. Thanks so much!

Now the [bad] spell has probably been broken. I'm looking forward to our telephone conversation later today. I am at Dr. Opfers's place because Aunt Margot is leaving on Tuesday, but through customer service I have had all incoming phone calls from 5:00 to 10:00 P.M. transferred to me here.

You've probably received our card by now. Vati was here Friday and Saturday (by now he is in Hamburg), and I was very happy about one thing in particular: He told me that you had behaved perfectly. Well—[no wonder] with your upbringing! He was very nice and would like to help me, but so far no permit has turned up. Yesterday evening we had a ladies' farewell at Mrs. Hirschbach's. All the women are leaving. So the only ones who will still be here next week are Miss Cenki, who figures on leaving in July, Miss Schwarze, in two years, and me. Mrs. Lessler and Miss Heine, who weren't there, will be saying good-bye on Tuesday.[5] And guess who is moving into my apartment: Mr. and Mrs. Marcus and one of their women friends (I can just see your faces). Miss Schn.[ackenburg] is leaving on March 1; she is looking for a room right now (she had to have all her teeth pulled—horrible). I am keeping the front room, and Marcus and company are getting the bedroom and Schnackchen's room. Mrs. Marcus will cook for me, too, and also clean my room. That way I'll save a lot of money, and I hope that it will still be comfortable here. What do you think of all this?

I'm in bed; you may have guessed that from my handwriting. But all week long I've felt pretty miserable (a cold and something else) and so I have to get a good rest.

I'll be happy to send you the books, dear Inge, but perhaps I can also send some for Mariönchen at the same time. So please let me know, my Little Macaroon.[6] It's good that you're learning Latin and that you're enjoying the music lessons. Only yesterday I realized once again how well off you are: Helga Horwitz, who was in your class, Marion, is in a foreign country (I don't know where, working on a farm for some farmers; she has to scrub floors, milk cows, and do the roughest sort of work. She can't eat so much as a crumb because the people there are so unmannerly and dirty). Aunt Irma is still in Vienna. I am giving Rolf the stamps. Who bought you the lamp shade? I am glad you're getting such good food; are you eating well, Marion? I'm not worried about Inge. I'm enclosing another picture. Please keep it and send me back the old one. I think these prints are much better. Even Vati asked me for one.

Would you like me to send you another little package? How are things going with B? It's 4:00 P.M. now. In three hours we'll be talking with one another; how wonderful! I can't wait!

I send many affectionate little kisses and a big hug for both of you sweeties. And after you've read this letter, give each other a big kiss because you love each other so much. I hope you continue to get along well.

Keep loving your faithful Mütterlein

Berlin/Wilm., April 20, 1939

My dearest children,

I received your nice letter today, and I also found your letter, dear little Marion, waiting for me when I came back from Vienna. I'm always happy when I get mail from you. Dear Kitten, I can understand your wanting to grow up more quickly just now, but with time that will take care of itself, and when you reach my age, it can't happen slowly enough. Ingelein, I can't send you my measurements today because it's already 11:30 at night and there's no one who can measure me; but I'll definitely do it in my next letter.

In the meantime, did Vati come to see you? Write me soon. Your excursions must have been nice, but why wasn't Marion allowed to go along? You danced, Ingelein—that's good; I'd like to dance again, too. Your game, Little Macaroon, is very interesting, and now I understand it, too, because you sent such a good sketch of it. I'm going to play it with the Latté children, because they have chips.

I am well. I still have a tan. Yesterday was the first day of school, and the children [in my class] were really glad that I was still their teacher. Today we had a day off (Hitler's birthday). The Lessler School is gone; the Goldschmidt School is moving into the [Lessler School] building on Kronbergstrasse. Marion Latté is going to go there until they emigrate; they'll probably be leaving soon.

Aunt Margot and Evchen have found jobs in London with a young couple who have a baby, and they are now very happy. Hochschilds have rented a six-room house in Philadelphia; Edgar can hardly write German anymore. Your report card is quite good, Marion. Didn't you get one, Inge? How is your French?

Have you gone swimming yet? Did Vati buy you bathing suits? If not, then it would be best if you tell Mr. Baruschke. I hope you weren't too immodest. And write and tell me sometime who your best friend is and why you picked her. I assume that you don't quarrel anymore, because when you live among total strangers, you should feel even closer to each other. I hope you love each other and help each other.

Write to me soon about everything and in detail. You know how happy I am to hear from you.

With tender love, many, many thousands of kisses,

Your Mutti

Berlin, June 19, 1939

My dearest children,

On Monday, when we spoke on the telephone, you told me that you had already started to write me a letter; I wonder where it is. But it was really nice to talk, wasn't it? I'm so glad that you like being there, in a peaceful environment that makes studying fun. If I could only get a glimpse of you! Tomorrow Mr. Baruschke will be coming to Berlin; I hope he will tell me a lot of good things about you. Have you heard about your vacation yet? I wrote to a hotel in Constance to ask whether they could and would take us, but I haven't had an answer yet. No word from Vati, either.

You asked about my going to England. It's not as easy as you think. Almost everyone, especially Aunt Margot, is very unhappy there. They have to work as "domestics" from 6:00 in the morning until 10:00 at night; they eat in the kitchen, and all day long they scrub and clean, and then when they have their day off on Wednesday or Thursday, they are either so tired that all they want to do is sleep, or they don't have enough money to do anything. They earn 15 pounds = 7

Reichsmark a week, which has to pay for shoes, carfare, beauty parlor, etc., so that they can't even go to the movies. And you know, I wouldn't be any closer to you there because one has to work as a "domestic" for two years, and don't think I'd get vacations the way one does teaching school. For the time being, I'm much better off here, and once we've seen one another during the vacations, we'll be able to put up with this separation a little longer, right? Nobody is really doing me any harm here.

I am permitted to keep my apartment because Vati is an Aryan and because of you; all the other [Jews] who live in Aryan houses have to move out, and Jews are not allowed to live in the neighborhoods around the Bayrischer Platz, Kurfürstendamm, and Potsdamer Strasse, etc. Heinz Wasserzug is leaving for England June 20; Marion and Rolf Latté, on the 27th, and their parents will follow shortly.

As you can see from the card we sent you yesterday, we were in the Grunewald.[7] I missed you very much. It just occurred to me that I was supposed to send you regards from Aunt Polly. She too is in England working as a "domestic" and very unhappy. Uncle Walther [*sic*] is in Shanghai, and he is dissatisfied also. Miss Rothschild, the pretty teacher from the Auguststrasse School who came to visit us once, is suffering the same fate. Miss Behrendt is moving to Australia from England.

I get along well with the Marcuses; he never shouts and is very calm. He now teaches at the Kaiserstrasse School. Dear Inge, please write to Dr. Erich Loewenthal, Küstrinerstrasse 14. He can't get it out of his head that you never said goodbye to him.

Did you get the package [I sent] in the meantime? Inge, the white dress shrank so much in the wash that it will probably fit you. You have to remove the red buttons each time and not sew them back on in the same place, but rather on both parts of the skirt. You probably noticed that. Dear Little Macaroon, this time I didn't send anything for you to wear, and although I am very sorry, there is no way I can send you the stamps. Vati agrees. I really regret not being able to do more for you.

Since I wrote the above, some days have passed. I see from

the card you and Vati sent me that you are together. Any news about the vacation? Ours starts on Wednesday. The hotel in Constance wrote to say they couldn't take us, but I have already written to another one. Please ask Daddy to let me know immediately. Write me a long letter soon. Affectionate regards and kisses and many hugs,

Your very loving Mutti

Oh, if only I could be in Vati's shoes and be with you, even for a moment!

Berlin/Wilm., August 14, 1939

My dearest children,

If I were to stick to our agreement, then I ought not to be writing you now, for you haven't written to me in a very, very long time. But mothers aren't like that. I'm not the only one who is surprised. Uncle Walter is, too. So please make up for it quickly and write to me and to him.

I wonder how you are. Is your eye getting better, Ingelein? And how are you, my Little Macaroon? I hope everything is all right with you, Ingelein. Please write to me next month, and if it [the eye] is really bad, then stay in bed for a day. Did you get the chain letter? I am well. As I write this there is lightning and thunder here; it's terrifying. Miss Kaphan told us today that she is going to Sweden on October 1 to become head of a Jewish children's home. She deserves this chance; I would like to do something like that, too. However, I think I have no choice but to go to England as a "domestic." My cousin Hermann said so, too, in a letter he wrote me from London. I'm afraid I'll be able to work here only until October. But no one knows for sure yet.

Vati will probably be back in Leipzig today.

Yesterday I had lunch at Aunt Irma's and then I had afternoon coffee and supper at the Lattés'. They are leaving soon.

Later in the evening I spent an hour with Uncle Walter, who is having a very hard time. Send him some chocolate, if you can. I enclose a voucher so that you can do it.[8]

Also, please write to the Kittlers; I think Uncle Heiner and Gerda have birthdays coming up. I'll write to them, too.

Since I promised to let you know whenever I buy something for myself, I should tell you that I bought two pairs of shoes (a brown pair and a black-and-white pair) on sale. And Mrs. Latté made a black hat for me; I'll try to draw a picture of it:

How do you like the way I look [in this picture]?

This is how the children in my class would draw me!

Well, now, may you get better soon (in writing letters to me). Best wishes and many, many kisses,

Your very loving Mutti

Berlin/Wilm., August 30, 1939
Rudolstädterstr. 104

My dearest children,

Don't you think it's been a very long time since you wrote to me?

Please, sit down right now and write me in detail all about yourselves.

I'm well. It's still quite warm here, but we're not getting any more time off because of the heat. Miss Hecht came for coffee on Saturday afternoon, a pleasant, cultured young woman. She told me a lot about you, and I now have a better picture of your life there. Mrs. Grelling called to say how sorry she was that her daughter cannot leave anymore, but I think that's only temporary. In any case we must be careful to make sure that nothing happens, especially when going swimming; I hope you know what I mean.[9]

Vati was here last Tuesday, but I think I wrote you about that already. Last Saturday I bought a dress for school and a smock; one needs a ration card for that now.

Uncle Walter bought me a fabulous radio; I can get all the stations, even Switzerland. You've got to let me know when Miss Serron is playing so that I can get to know her, too. You can probably picture Uncle Walter and me sitting in front of the radio every evening. Last night we heard "Tosca" with Gigli from Rome.

Tomorrow I am going to the Emigration Office of the [Jewish] Community to find out about things, but for the moment nothing is likely to happen.

Have you heard from Vati? I am going to write to him right after I finish this. Then I'm going with the Marcuses to the Neufelds'; the Birnbaums are going to be there, too. If I keep saying no to their invitation, they'll think I'm too stuck-up.

Ingelein, I won't be able to buy you the material for your dress. You'll have to try to get it there. I'm sure they have it in Geneva.

I had postcards made from the photographs of you taken near Kipho. I bought frames and now I have you both on my desk. You look so happy and joyful that it simply won't do for me to be sad. But when it does happen, I give you each a kiss, and then everything is all right again, because I have to be so very glad that you are there. (The Lattés are in England.)

Write to me right away. Please, please!!

My love and kisses and many many hugs.

Your very loving Mutti

Berlin/Wilm., September 4, 1939

My dearest children,

I don't know when and if this letter will reach you, but I'll write anyway and tell you that I'm all right. Don't worry about me. Whatever happens, we have to take it as it comes, and we can't change anything. It's all destiny! So far everything has turned out all right, hasn't it? I am very sad, though, not to be getting any mail from you. Still, knowing that you are there is bound to help me. I haven't heard anything from Vati, either; I hope I will hear from him soon.

There is no school for us until further notice. As a housewife, one isn't bored, of course, especially in times like these. But having only yourself to take care of isn't nice. Uncle Walter visits me often, and this is good because I would be even more unhappy if I were constantly alone.

Did you receive my last letter? Wasn't it wonderful that we were able to talk on the telephone? But your voices sounded so sad. Has your school started again?

If I don't hear from you by Sunday, I'll try to call you again Sunday evening or Monday morning.

Friends who are still here are: Uncle Walter, Aunt Irma—we went there for coffee yesterday—the Bauers, the Beneckes, and Mrs. Goldschmidt, period.

Write to me even if the mail service is unreliable. Perhaps some of your letters will get through.

I think of you very, very often.

My love and many, many kisses and hugs.

Your loving Mutti

Berlin/Wilm., November 26, 1939

My dearest children,

I have trouble writing today because I have neuritis in my right arm. Nevertheless, I wanted you to get a letter from me. Last week Marion was a particularly diligent letter-writer, but Inge was very lazy—only Aunt Irma and Uncle Walter heard from her. You see, I know a lot about you, dear Inge. But why don't you write to me? You have so much to tell! How did you make the Arabian costume? Why don't you take photographs of each other? I really would like to know how my daughters look. And what did you do that evening? Sit down, dear Ingelein, and write me a detailed letter. Vati will probably come [to Berlin] next week, and he will tell me all about you.

Mrs. Hourath called. I wonder why there are no letters from the Hochschilds and the Lattés. How did your last school assignments work out? You seem to be writing very little about school and what you are doing there. Will you be promoted at Easter time? Into which grade? What did the medical examination show?

It was sweet of you, dear Marion, to send me suggestions for our performance, but we thought of something on our own: Some children want to celebrate Hanukkah using their dolls. They improvise quite freely. A poor man comes along and they give him all the food they have. But then their mother gives them more food. We intersperse this with German and Hebrew poems and songs. One of the children sings in Turkish, another in Polish, a third in French.

My Regina, who looks like Frank, left for Palestine yesterday, without her parents; I went to the train station [to see her off] and gave her your Oblaten because she now plays "Steckbilder" all the time.[10] I gave your doll carriage to Lissa Bauer; is that all right with you? By the time your children are ready for such things, the carriage will be old-fashioned. Marionka, you write that chocolate isn't all that wonderful! In November we got 100 grams, in December we'll be getting 200 grams. Do you know how much, or actually how little, that is? You'll make me very happy by sending me chocolate, butter, and coffee. The doctor thinks that my neuritis, an inflammation of the nerve, is caused by my not having enough fat padding. Dear Marion, I don't understand why you are sewing the scarf for Susi closed. Isn't one allowed to send scarves? I could use one to go with the brown coat, but a warm one because it is bitterly cold here.

Why do you move around so often? I don't think that's very good. How far have you gotten with your sweaters? Perhaps I'll go to Ahlem (for a convention of English teachers) from December 12 to January 3, 1940. That way I won't be so terribly aware of the fact that you're not here with me.

Please write very soon with lots of details. Many kisses and embraces (many cuddly hugs).

Your loving Mutti

Hanover/Limmer, December 27, 1939
Gartenbauschule [Horticultural School]/Ahlem

My dearest children,

Today you're going to get a detailed report from here, even though I haven't heard from you since I arrived. My thoughts are with you often in spite of the fact that I am very busy. I spent Christmas Eve with the children at this place (30 are staying here during the vacation; at other times there are 120). The children sang Hebrew and Yiddish songs, and I knew that you would be singing Christmas carols. That made me feel very peculiar. But it doesn't matter what one sings and what one celebrates. What is important is that what we do and think is decent and good, and even though I sing one thing here and you sing something else there, the tie that binds us is just as close as before. I know what you think and how you feel, and you know the same of me. Please send me a complete description of everything you're doing. Did my little presents arrive in time?

Was Vati there? I want to know everything, everything.

And now, let me tell you about what is going on here. I arrived with a colleague from Berlin at noon on Friday. All the other participants are from other cities: Düsseldorf, Essen, Karlsruhe, Sudetenland, Königsberg, and so on. There are about forty of us (men and women) ranging in age from the mid-twenties to the late fifties. All the women (twenty) sleep in *one* room. Along the walls are *Handsteine* (do you still remember what that is?) with running cold water.[11] At night there's giggling and gossiping just as in a regular girls' boarding school (until one of us turns sensible and sees to it that things quiet down).

Now I'll describe a typical day for you. At 7:30 my alarm goes off. We—the young ones (they think I'm somewhere between twenty and twenty-six years old)—get up, splash some water on our faces, and put on our track suits. Then it's outside for "gymnastics." There are five women and five men (I'm second best and that includes cross-country running, so you can imagine what the others are like). Then we really

wash up and get dressed. At 8:45 we have coffee and a huge
buttered roll. The first class is at 9:15: grammar in three sec-
tions; I'm in the second section. First we write a practice piece;
then written exercises. At 12:30 we have lunch, and after that
until 4:00 we can rest or go for a walk, or do schoolwork. At
4:30 there's conversation, then an American instructor comes
in and gives a lecture, and at 7:00 we eat supper. After that
there is another lecture or English songs or a practice class.
From 9:30 on, we talk to one another, play games, or dance—
of course only English is spoken. For a change I'm not reading
any newspapers, and that's wonderful. Naturally it's tempting
to laugh at the way different people speak the language, and
sometimes I giggle as though I were my own daughter.

It's noontime now, and after I've finished this letter, I'm
going to Hanover with some of my colleagues. The conference
ends on January 2, 1940. The final evening here we are having
a graduation party; I hope it will be nice. New Year's Eve we'll
probably have a little party, too. I don't think I can telephone
you, but I'll try.

Please write soon and in great detail. Regards to Vati. Best
wishes and kisses.

Your also-a-student,

Mutti

❖

1940
JANUARY 19–NOVEMBER 16

Berlin/Wilm., January 19, 1940

My dearest grown-up birthday child,

My thoughts wander back in time to a year ago when I was still able to give you a birthday kiss in person, to take you in my arms, and whatever my lips didn't tell you, my eyes did. And as I talk to you now, please hold my picture in your hand, or set it up in front of you so that I can be really, really close to you. Dear Inge, grown-up Inge—I wish you all things that are good, beautiful, kind, and warm. I would like to express my deep mother's love in these words. When you were younger, you sometimes caused me sorrow and worry, but since then you've become more sensible and you've brought me only joy. I have boundless faith in you and would go through fire to prove my faith in you and the belief I have that you are not capable of lying or doing wrong. And for that reason I know that things must and will always go well for you. Up to now you never had to choose between right and wrong. The older one gets, the more frequently we have to confront this problem, but I know you will always choose to do what's right. I also have absolute faith in your attitude toward me. But we must try to speak with each other very soon. I am trying everything to make that possible, but at the moment it seems doubtful that I'll succeed. I miss you both very, very much!

Do you like your briefcase? Things like that aren't available here anymore, and I paid a great deal of money for it (22.50 RM). I mention this, even though it isn't the polite thing to do, just so that you won't wonder why you got only one present. *Die Unbekannte* [the book *The Unknown*] isn't

17

available just now; when it does become available again, I'll send it to you.

And please be kind to Marion. Make believe it's me.

And now, dear child, may you become a good, kind, honest, and dependable human being, and don't ever forget that I love you and Marion more than anything else in the world.

Many, many kisses and embraces.

Your Mutti

Berlin/Wilm., February 2, 1940

My dearest children,

Well, now you've made up for everything. Your dear letters made me very happy. It's a good sign that my present arrived on time, even though I sent my letters earlier. Did you get my letter from Ahlem? You never answered it! You probably haven't been making the proper use of the portfolios. These are not writing cases for letters; they're briefcases that you use like attaché cases to carry books and music, and in the front there is a place where you put your notebooks. Students use these briefcases a lot. I would have liked to have bought one for myself, too, but I felt it was too expensive. I thought, as you go from your room to class, you could put all your things into them. Please let me know how that worked out.

It is bitterly cold here— -20° C [-4° F]. There's no school; we meet only on Wednesdays in the unheated rooms to check the homework assignments and to hand out new ones. This worked out well for me because I was pretty sick. But now everything is all right again, and I am recuperating. I look better, too.

I now wear my hair the same way you do, Inge, and you, too, little Marionka. I think people would really take us for three sisters. If only we were together again! We must never lose sight of this as a common goal in everything we do. As for what you wrote, dear Inge, in your last letter. I think time is on our side. No one knows what tomorrow will bring. Study, work, and never lose sight of your goal; that is what I do. Vati knows just as little about what is going to happen as you and I. I want you to stay in school as long as possible because I have the feeling that you are happy there and that you are learning many useful things. And our goal, now and always, must be to be reunited as soon as possible. The love we feel for one another will show us the right way. We have to stay faithful to each other—you know that I always am, and I know that you will be, too. There's still lots of time to decide whether you will study medicine or join the publishing house, and until then, plenty of water will flow under the bridge. Time will be on our side!

I'm happy that you enjoy music so much. I feel a tremendous longing for it, but I have *no* opportunities here anymore. I love and treasure Beethoven above all. How wonderful that you can enjoy all this. You wouldn't have the opportunity here.

Marion, please be kind to Carola. It's terrible to lose one's father at such a young age.

You ask about sending me things. Of course I *can use everything;* but please send it "registered mail." Three little packages that Vati sent me got lost. Life is not easy for us here. Well! So you, Inge, got genuine silk stockings from Marion! What a major present, and soon my daughters will be more elegant than their mother.

Unfortunately, I cannot write you a letter in English. I won't tell you why, just as Inge wrote the other day. Is your place well heated? Aunt Irma just telephoned. Her apartment is very cold, and she's coming over tomorrow to warm up.

Marion, your report card is quite good, but history and biology could be better. Did you not get a report card, Inge, or were your grades bad? Yes, go ahead and give your best shoes to Carola.

Inge, dear, in a few days I'll be sending you some books. Here we're also wearing only hoods. I made myself one from my green scarf. What did you do on Sunday? Why were you separated from Susi? Did the skis that Vati sent arrive? Did you get any mail from the Kittlers? I think the present (15 postage stamps) is wonderful. Here you get only *one* reply coupon with every letter. What is "the V" that Brother Grelling gave you? I can't imagine what that is.

Well, enough for today, I can't write any more.

Warmest heartfelt wishes, kisses, and hugs. I love you very, very much and miss you.

Your
Mutti

Please send the Lattés the pictures of the Bauers' children when you write to them; [Lattés] would like to hear from them sometime.

Berlin, February 8, 1940

Dearest Marion,

This morning I received your card dated the 2nd and just now, at noon, your long letter. I'll write a long detailed answer later. For the moment let's hope that my application will be approved.

Mr. and Mrs. Meseritz were here for three days. Susi is in Peru, happily married, and Ursel lives in Hollywood and is working in a factory that makes ties. She could have gotten married already (she's twenty years old), but first she wants to arrange for her parents to come over. Isn't that touching? But Mr. Meseritz is nearly blind.

I'm well again. I'm glad that you have such a good command of French now, but before you used to like dancing so much. Or do you still like to dance and just don't like the teacher? Are you using the briefcases the way I suggested in my letter? It really doesn't matter; the important thing is that you like them. Did Inge receive both my birthday letters?

Many fond kisses and hugs, dear child.

Your
Mutti

March 1940

My dearest child,

I just received your nice letter dated February 24 and want to answer you immediately since we're still on a "coal vacation." The [real] vacation starts on March 20; I don't think we will be working from now till then. But we have to make out report cards, and some children have to be left back. We've hardly had any school since January. See how hard being a teacher is.

I'd like you to send an *urgent* letter to Uncle Paul *immediately,* asking him whether he can find anyone to help me. I applied for a quota number at the American Consulate. But even if I get one, I will surely have to wait ten years [for the number to come up]. I don't have an affidavit, either, and I really don't know what to do. But I *have* to emigrate as quickly as possible. Ingelein, please use all your wits and put as much urgency into your letter as possible; do you understand?

Here nothing has changed. I am well, but I have to see to it that I get to another country. You don't have to worry about me, but please write to Uncle Paul with the utmost urgency. The day before yesterday Renate's parents were here. Do write her a long letter sometime (Kastanienallee 34). Yesterday the Birnbaums and Dr. Loewenthal were here and they send you regards.

Try a little harder in mathematics, dear Inge, because I'd like to see you get into the Unterprima [the eighth year in secondary school]. None of us knows what will happen and whether Vati will be able to pay the tuition much longer. I haven't had any word from him.

I'd like to tell you once again, be happy and learn *as much as you can. You'll never experience such a carefree, happy time again!*

I went to the Kulturbund [the Jewish Cultural Association] with Mr. Goldstaub on Saturday afternoon to see *Taming of the Shrew,* by Shakespeare. Hanna made the costumes and decorations. It was very nice and funny. Do you know the play?

I haven't had an answer to my Swiss application. Tomorrow I'll go to the consulate.

Please write immediately to Uncle Paul—S.O.S. You can show this letter to Marion, and ask her to show you hers.

Fond hugs, kisses, and cuddling.

Your loving
Mutti

Berlin, March 27, 1940

My dearest Inge,

According to my tally, it's your turn to get a long, detailed letter from me, and so I am about to make that happen. I'm anxious to know what Uncle Paul's answer will be. In the meantime, I've received an application waiting number for America; it even includes you two, because one never knows what turns life will take.

Nothing special has happened here, and you mustn't worry about me. But I don't think I can stay in Germany. You know how I feel about you, and of course without you I wouldn't migrate to another part of the world. We'll have to wait and see! We can only try to stay well and study, study! The day may soon come when *you will have to earn a living.* That's to be expected. So use this time well—be happy, stay in good health, and learn both practical and academic things, and if on top of that you can also cultivate the arts, then that is your very special good fortune.

Vati told me he sent you some excellent books. I've read *Raubfischer auf Hellas;* after you've read it, let me know what you think of it. I'll try to get you a volume of collected poetry. I couldn't arouse any enthusiasm in Vati about violin lessons. Let's wait a while with that. I'm sure you have more urgent things to do.

I'll get the book for the Lattés and send it to you. Mr. Goldstaub is joining his brother in the U.S.A. He has wrapped up almost all his affairs here and intends to leave from Genoa on May 4. For him this is wonderful; for those of us who have to stay behind, it's not so nice. Soon there'll be only old people left here. This afternoon I had a visit from your teacher in Hamburg. Her name used to be Miss Backrad. (Do you still remember her? She taught physical education, needlework and sewing, and drawing.) She is now Mrs. Krayn, and she was here with her husband. They want to go to Shanghai.

I feel fine. I went to Dresden for a few (four) days with a friend from Altona. There are no vacations now; we have to be in school every day at noon to check over the homework assignments and hand out new ones. On Friday the students get their report cards (two of my children are being left back and one child is being transferred to a remedial school). On Monday the new school year begins (we're all moving on to the third grade). I'm being promoted along with the children.

I received your letters of (March) 10 and 15, and this morning your postcard of March 18. Just now I heard the lid on the mailbox clattering—it was Marion's card of the 19th, and now I'm worried. What's the matter with your intestines? Write to me *immediately.* Diarrhea? Ate too much? I'm going to take this letter to work with me, and on the way I'll stop by to pick up another reply coupon. Unfortunately, you can only get one at a time. Please write to me with the next mail. I'll write to Marion soon. Warmest wishes and tight hugs.

Your faithful and loving
Mutti

Berlin/Wilm., April 3, 1940

My dearest children,
Today, I'll write to both of you for a change. If you're going to have an argument about the reply coupon, you can send me a joint letter, but I think that's all "tempi passati." You asked whether I save your letters. Of course I do! As soon as I've read one, I put it into a file, and I keep careful track of everything. I wish I could show them to you.

Bit by bit, but ever so slowly, spring is arriving. Today I was walking through Konstanzer Strasse when I saw the first snowdrops, and I thought, if only Inge and Marion were here with me. Then all three of us would have enjoyed these flowers and we would have shouted, "Look there, and there, and there." And then I missed you very, very much. But I have to be sensible and tell myself over and over again, "Here I couldn't provide as nice a place for you to live in as you have there." Being sensible can sometimes be very hard. You probably know that, too, from experience. We are still not on a regular schedule. Today I worked three and one-half hours, and tomorrow I have to travel that long distance for only a half-hour class. The classrooms are still too chilly.

In all my life I have never worked so little as in the last quarter year; I've gotten quite rusty. Inge, dear, I found a violin and a flute. I'll try to send them to you; I'm not sure whether it will work. You'll have to have the violin fixed there (have strings put on, etc.). Since you're lending the flute to someone, the boy ought to have it fixed.

And now to get to your letters. Marion, I'm happy with every letter you write, and I would like to know about everything—what you think and what you do. But sometimes the tone of your letters sounds so impudent that I have a hunch you may be quite cheeky to your teachers. Am I wrong? Please think about your behavior and let me know the results. On the subject of examinations: I'm very sorry to hear that Brigitte failed, and the fact that the boy didn't pass, either, makes me wonder. I think, and I'm afraid, that you two are not working hard enough. I really don't want to have the same thing happen to you sometime, and I think Vati, too, would be very disappointed if that were to happen; so get to work before it's too late.

How much I would have liked to send you something for Easter, but I myself have nothing—that's all I can say about that. But from your letter, dear Marion, I see that you had all kinds of sweets and that there was a joyful celebration. I spent a few days in Dresden with a woman colleague whom I met in

Ahlem. It was lovely. The city of Dresden has splendid archi-
tecture. Unfortunately, we were not allowed to go into the
museums, etc.

Our new school year starts on April 1. What grade are you
in now? I am the teacher for the third grade, and in addition to
that I teach twelve hours of physical education. Since the class
teacher for the children who are just beginning school was
sick, I had to make the welcoming speech to the new parents
and children. It went quite well, and actually your ears must
have been ringing because I told them about when you first
started school, etc. You know me!

Uncle Walter was here last night. He is quite all right.

Tell me, do you go on "summer time" there, too? On April 1
at 2:00 A.M. all the clocks here were set forward to 3:00. Because
of that, we now turn the lights on later in the evenings.

Today I'm going to the movies at 2:30 — a funny time, isn't
it? But since "we" are not permitted to be on the street after
8:00 P.M., there are now two shows for "us" — at 2:30 and 5:00
(but the 5:00 P.M. show is already sold out). I think it's been
three months since I was there last; it's so far away.

Now it's time for me to go to school (11:30–12:00).

Warmest regards and thousands of hugs and kisses. I long
for you.

Your
Mutti

Berlin, June 22, 1940

My dearest children,

Thanks for your lovely cards and letters; please don't
worry if I don't write as often as I used to, but we have been
told not to write too often. In spite of that, I am of course
doing whatever I can. In addition, dear Inge, I am allowed to
send you only letters I have written myself and so I'll have to

tell you what Gerd wrote from Leipzig. He has scarlet fever and has to stay in bed for six weeks, but he's doing all right. He was very happy with your thoughtful present. By now Susi has probably written to you. She was able to see for herself that I'm all right. I hope she'll visit me again the next time she comes to Berlin.

Our vacation starts on Friday, and you can imagine how sad I am that you're not going to be here. The Marcuses are going to visit relatives. And I will probably have to stay here since I don't know where else to go. Maybe I'll still find something. Vati wrote to me from Leipzig.

Many of the things you say in your letters make me very happy. Dear Marion, I'm glad you realize that modesty is a great and worthwhile virtue, and I hope that you will never be arrogant, conceited, or immodest, because all three of these qualities are a sign of stupidity; and you certainly aren't stupid, are you? All truly great people are simple and modest because they realize how little they know, how little they can accomplish—only half-educated and stupid people think that they always have to be in on everything, that they know it all.

Your dream about the bear is attributable to swimming and is probably due to the fact that your bedcovers weren't on straight.

In a little while I have to go to school, but I'll write again soon. I just want to answer one more question: Yes, I'm outdoors a lot (Wannsee, Treptow, etc.) with my colleagues.

Have you finished reading the *Leiden* [*Sorrows of Young Werther*]? I'd be interested to hear what you think of it.

Please continue to write often. Your letters make me very happy and put my mind at ease.

Warmest kisses and many tight hugs,

Your loving
Mutti

Strausberg, July 26, 1940
3 Weinbergstrasse near Liegat

My dearest children,

It's raining. I sit at the open window, and whenever I'm not writing I look out at the garden, the woods, and the lake, but everything looks dreary today. Still, it probably has to be like that to make us really appreciate the sun and the light. I wonder where you are right now. In Zurich? Do you still remember last year when you were allowed to do the shopping and the cooking? I haven't had any news from you in a long while; perhaps there'll be something from you in today's mail, which is delivered very late and only once a day.

I'm fine. I've gotten accustomed to the old ladies. They can really be quite jolly and they treat me like a little girl. In the evenings the four of us play 66 [a card game]. It's a lot of fun and helps me forget my troubles. I swim a lot; the lake is about 350 meters [1,000 feet] across, and I swim to the other shore, take a walk in the woods, do a few exercises, and then I swim back. This is what I do in the mornings. In the afternoons I go for a walk and then I do some rowing or paddling. So you see I'm really on vacation. Sunday Aunt Irma is coming with her mother, and today someone from Berlin is coming for a visit. Sad to say, on Wednesday I have to go home again because school starts on Thursday. The public school children are on vacation until August 23, and your vacation is even longer, isn't it?

I received a long letter, and some photos, from the Kittlers. I think you will be getting them, too, except for the one of Uncle Heiner. Well, children, it's not nice that at the moment I know so little about what you're doing. Please write me a long, detailed letter. Dear Inge, did you hear anything from Susi? Is Rosy staying there permanently or only for the vacation? Are you staying with Miss Kempf or with the Enderlins? Are all your things in good shape, or do you need new things? You also were going to let me know how tall you are!

I am glad that Inge lost two pounds. When I got married I weighed ninety-nine pounds, but I was not as tall as you.

And now, dear children, enjoy your vacation. Our greatest wish must be that we will all be together again soon.

Many tight hugs and kisses,

Your loving
Mutti

Berlin, August 24, 1940

My dearest Inge,

Thank you for your letter of the 9th and the card dated the 13th of August. You promised me a *very* long, detailed letter; still, I can see from the few lines you wrote that you enjoyed Zurich. What sort of person is Miss Kempf and what does she look like? I wrote briefly to her today thanking her for the hospitality she showed you. Did you talk about me? And so school is about to start for you again; oh well, the vacation was certainly long enough. For weeks it's been rainy and cold here, in contrast to the weather you're having. It's really essential that we have a few more nice days before the bad winter starts—I hope it will be milder than last year.

I see Eva Cohn at school now and then. She is attending home economics courses here. Recently a girl from your class talked to me at the movies, but I don't know her name. All the Lessler School students are gone. Miss Anker hopes to be able to go to the U.S.A. soon.

Is it definite that Vati is coming? He hasn't written to me about it yet. I'm glad you had a letter from Gerd. Is he still in the army?

What kind of dresses did you make in Zurich? Which ones did you alter? Did you also buy some ready-made clothes?

I am well. School continues. Beginning in October, all classes of the same grade level are being consolidated; then I'll have 47 children in one class. But it's better to have a lot of work than none, right?

How is your French? And English? I take English twice a week, but I'm not pleased with my present teacher (yes, things like that do happen), but after September 1 I'll have a different one whom I like a lot.

So, my dear child, please write me a long, detailed letter, and also tell me about your friends, boys as well as girls. Many affectionate kisses and hugs,

Your loving
Mutti

Berlin, September 1, 1940

My dearest little Marion,

I intended to write to you every day this week, but four teachers are absent from school, and I had to do a lot of substituting. I'm writing now in a pretty uncomfortable position, but what matters is the fact that I'm writing and what I'm writing and not how. First of all, I want to tell you and Inge that I'm all right; I don't sleep much, but I feel well. Our school is in session continuously—no breaks. Unfortunately, after October 1 we *won't have a telephone anymore;* Vati and his people are allowed to keep theirs.

I miss you terribly, but there's nothing I can do about that, and we have to keep hoping that we'll be reunited again soon, very soon. I'm going to have some photographs taken in all sorts of settings, because I don't want you to forget me. This last sentence makes me very sad.

You complain that you can't express yourself well; I don't think that's true. I understand what you mean, and I'm happy to see that you can express so clearly what you think and feel. Yes, please write to me about your conversation with the boy. Your principle "Noli me tangere" is quite correct and important, and I'm glad that this is how you feel. I'm sure you talked about love—yes—this is a difficult subject; most grown-ups are unable to deal with it. The most beautiful and purest love is, and always has been, the love between a mother and her child.

Of course both of you ought to have good friends, and when you reach the appropriate age, you ought to get married—because old maids are dreadful. But for the time being, get involved in art, music, science, and nature. I'm glad you are reading such good books, but I'm terribly sorry that we can't read together in spite of the fact that I'm familiar with most of the books (such as *Gösta Berling* [by Selma Lagerlöf]). Still, I would read them again if we could do it together. Just imagine that we are sitting on the balcony or in our usual corner and one of us is reading aloud while the other two are sewing or darning; we'd discuss all our problems as they come up, and in between we'd nibble something sweet or eat some fruit. Can you imagine sitting on my lap and snuggling the way you used to do? You write that you scarcely know yourself. Almost everybody feels that way. I'm glad that you can observe and criticize yourself. You should always begin with yourself; then you will not be unfair to other people.

I am not allowed to send long letters, so I'll write you another time about what you said about Vati. But you are right, and that will have to suffice for today. I'm infinitely sorry that you cannot discuss things with Inge. I hope that that will improve as you both get older.

My dear child, many affectionate hugs and kisses,

Your loving
Mutti

I'm saving all your letters.

Berlin, October 3, 1940

My dearest Inge,

Today's letter will again be long and detailed. But won't you at least please share with Marion the most important things in it. Georg was here yesterday afternoon and this morning, and I liked him very much.[12] His manner, his behavior, his way of thinking are refined and speak of culture and great modesty. "He doesn't put on airs," and I like that. He brought me some beautiful flowers and we really had a pleasant conversation. I, too, think he's good-looking, a bit gangly still, but he has a fine face. Naturally, he told me a lot about you; actually he has given me the clearest picture so far of what you're like now. I also have the feeling that he knows you very well, your virtues as well as your faults. I hope that he'll soon come to see you and tell you about me. (A close acquaintance of mine, Mr. Heinz Landau, also had a chance to meet him and thought he was very nice.)

From Georg's description, I gather that you, dear Inge, are getting to resemble me more and more, in character and in temperament. It's really essential that we get to talk to each other soon so that you won't make the same mistakes I once made. I'm anxious to know what you discussed with Vati with regard to Easter, but after talking to Georg, I am even more convinced that the Zurich plan is not a good one. Of course I realize the difficulties involved in doing your Abitur in Gland.[13] Please write me exactly what you discussed, and don't make any final decisions before you hear from me.

I was very happy with your last letter, above all the part that says you are now getting closer to Marion. We have to cure her of her arrogant attitude, because it's a sign of stupidity. You can tell her that I said that because I'll write her the same thing.

I'll send you a Bible at the first opportunity; nor do I object if you attend religious instruction, because the more you *know*, the better. I have often talked to you and written to you about my own position on religion. You must become good human beings, then you will be religious, but I don't want you to commit yourselves *dogmatically* in any way, that is, to join a specific religious community.

How nice it would be if I could see the new nightgown! It sounds as though it turned out really well. Would you like to make one for me, too? I could really use it. And you know my size etc. (I weigh 112 pounds). And you? What did Vati get you? I was sad to hear that your bicycles ended up like that!

And you know how hard I worked to earn the money for them (Schwarzwald?).

I was terribly sorry that I did not meet Mr. Baruschke. I really miss not having a telephone. But before this, he always let me know he was coming a few days ahead of his arrival. It would have taken me only an hour to get to Berlin from Strausberg. Please thank Miss Mettler for her letter; I assume this is all right.

Soon I'll write you again about my work at school, which has changed quite a bit.

I hope you continue to be my dear, brave, and good little kitten. Affectionate kisses,

Your loving
Mutti

Berlin, October 16, 1940

My dearest child,

Your detailed letter made me tremendously happy. More than anything, it shows how much confidence you have in me. I won't let you down. We are on vacation until the 28th, and so I have time and leisure to send you a lengthy reply. But first I want to tell you that we are no longer in our beautiful school building. Yesterday we moved into an old house, but we already have to move out of there too. Yes, indeed—no comment needed. Now we don't know where we will be teaching, and there are forty-six children in my class.

But now, about you. Marion wrote me that Georg will be coming to Berlin. Unfortunately, I don't have a telephone anymore, but somehow he'll find a way to get in touch, and then I'll invite him to stop by. I like his letters very much; he seems mature, sensible, and kind. As for your question, I can only say that I find nothing amiss in your having several boyfriends. On the contrary, I think it's only natural and appropriate. After all, you're not Ruth Neufeld, thank God, thinking only of getting married. That would be very foolish. One can never have enough good friends; each of them should of course know that he's not the only one—in the first place, they'll all be much nicer to you (competition), and in the second place, none of them will take liberties. I know very well what you're afraid of, and I ask you with all my heart, don't let any of them get too close. Don't let them kiss you, Kitten, not even in fun. You can be pals and good friends, but the boys have to know exactly where you draw the line. You should seem neither too easy to get nor too proud or conceited. I still remember what my mother said to me (on the grounds of Eppendorf Hospital), and I was twenty-seven years old before Vati kissed me for the first time. You don't have to wait that long, but it will happen soon enough. I'm happy to hear about your friendships. I'll answer Gerd's letter within the next few days, and I'm looking forward to Georg's visit. This is the way it should be—after all, I want to be your good and true friend.

I have to say I'm sorry that Brigitte and all the others failed; it doesn't speak well for the school. I'd like to spare you and us this fiasco, but I can't drum up any enthusiasm for your Zurich plan, for reasons you already know. Perhaps I can talk with Vati before he leaves for Switzerland. Maybe you can find another way. What is Brigitte going to do now? Please describe Mrs. Stucki for me.

Are Miss M. and Hannele not being nice to you? I can't understand that. Do you spend much time with Marion? Please take care of her and act as my surrogate. A kind word to her will surely do wonders.

Oh well—we would talk about all these things if we could be together! Believe me, I need you two as much as you need me.

With *much* love,

Your best friend and Mutti

Berlin, November 11, 1940

My dearest Mariönchen,

I wonder if Georg has already been to see you? And what did he tell you? It was a good thing that he visited me, because he really told me a lot about you since he knows you both so well and is almost as fond of you as a brother. I liked him very much because he is refined, reserved, and modest. There is nothing boastful or superficial about him. It was almost as if some part of you were here, and I came to feel a little closer to you or you to me.

Brigitte's detailed letter also gave me a lot of information. But all the oral and written reports have something in common: you are too arrogant, both inwardly and externally. The more someone knows and the more important someone is, the simpler and more modest he is. And Kitten, be yourself, be natural and unaffected. There was a time, when I was your age, when I, too, was affected and artificial. Then, one of my mother's friends said to me, "You don't even know the right words to express yourself." You see, I still remember what she said, exactly, and then things improved, and I became almost the opposite, so that sometimes you could have accused me of being too natural! Don't you agree?

But everybody says you work hard and you have become more meticulous; you probably don't have a close girlfriend. Brigitte is no doubt gone by now, and she was too old for you anyway! Whom do you like most, not counting Inge, of course? I have the feeling that the two of you are getting closer all the time. For me that would be the nicest and also the most natural thing. I also think that your talents are so different that you complement each other very well.

I'm glad you had such a good birthday celebration. Ah, how I would have liked to have been there! That whole day I yearned to be with you—but then that's the case all the time. You wrote that I was going to get something good. Well, I've been eagerly looking forward to it, but nothing has arrived. I hope you've received the thing Georg was bringing you. Don't put it in a closet without mothballs or on a painted hanger—otherwise the moths will get it.

Is Vati still there? I haven't heard from him in a long time.

I have to go to school now, so I will finish this quickly. I hope you continue being my brave, sweet, dear girl. Many kisses and hugs.

Your loving
Mutti

Did the "Prellwitz" book arrive?

The publisher was supposed to have mailed it to you. What books did Vati give you, and what did you buy in the way of clothes? Write me about everything. I wrote these last sentences on the S-Bahn [the city railway].

Berlin, November 16, 1940

My dearest Inge,

All week long there has been no news from you, and I was feeling quite sad. Then today I was virtually flooded with mail and I'm so happy. I was awakened by the clatter of the mail slot and found two letters from you. At noon I received a special-delivery letter from Georg; it took only two and one-half days to get here (so, if you want to send me something quickly, use special delivery; it costs 60 cts). And around 3:00 P.M. the wonderful package arrived. Really, my heart can scarcely endure so much joy.

Well now, turning to your nice letter. I know that you and Marion love me almost as much as I love you and that you continue to keep faith with me as I with you, but this separation has been going on for too long and I simply have to see you again soon. Of course I'm very happy that you are getting along well with Vati. You know that I really hoped this would happen, but what would be terrible for me, for example, would be the thought that you might be somewhere in Germany staying with Vati and not with me. But that's probably not under discussion!? Why don't you write and tell me what's being planned? So far Vati has not told me anything.

You were also going to tell me all about your conversation with him, but so far you haven't. And I waited all week for it. Please, do it.

I had to laugh about the permanent wave! Don't you know your Mutti anymore, Kitten? I have naturally wavy hair, no permanent wave, and I wear my hair in a very simple style: a diagonal part and curls at the back. Did Georg think I looked too fashionable? I use hardly any makeup for obvious reasons, and I really don't think that our tastes are all that different. Up to this point we've always been in agreement! What could you possibly be wearing that I would not approve of?

It makes me unhappy to hear again that you and Marion aren't getting along. Can't you change that? Both of you ought to give in a little! Yes, this really worries me.

You asked who Mr. Landau is. Well, we met in the English course. He is fifty-five years old and used to be a pharmacist. He is no longer allowed to work because he is Jewish. He is a decent, quiet, intelligent, and cultivated man. You know that pharmacists, like doctors, have to study at a university, and he has a great deal of general knowledge. He is reserved and modest, very precise, always neat, and well-dressed. He is not handsome, but he has an intelligent, spiritual face. He is an open, honest, decent human being—and that is what really matters. We spend a lot of time together, and if I don't want to be alone, I don't have to be. I'm sure you like that idea. He has a sister in San Francisco who sent him an affidavit. His quota number is coming up, and it's possible that he will soon be able to go to America. He wants to do everything possible for me, but for the time being nothing can be done since I don't have an affidavit. Perhaps once he's over there, he'll be able to get one for me.

But don't worry, my foremost thoughts center around you, and whatever course my life may take, you are *always first in my heart.* But since you are not here, it is good for me to have someone with whom I can share the joys and sorrows of life. Otherwise I couldn't bear it; I'm sure you understand that. He would like to meet you, and I think you'd get along well together. He is a combination of my father, my brother

Hermann, and a good friend. But for the time being I am not thinking of marriage. Don't tell Vati that I wrote you about this. I will do so myself. Did Georg talk to Marion about Mr. L., too? I've now written to you as I would to my closest girlfriend, right?

The things in the package are wonderful. Did you and Marion send it off together? It's good that one is permitted to send packages again. Many thanks. I had to pay 1.60 RM customs duty, but I was glad to do that.

Well, I hope you're pleased with your Mutti-cum-girlfriend!

Write me soon, many kisses and tight cuddly hugs.

Your Mutti

1941

JANUARY 19–DECEMBER 29

Berlin, January 19, 1941

My dearest Inge,

You had to wait longer for my promised letter than I intended, but I haven't been feeling well, not at all, and I looked dreadful. Now, though, I'm my "old" self again. I probably wrote you that I ran into a door in the dark and it caused a veritable horn, almost a second nose, to swell up on my forehead. The swelling spread all over my face and gave me bad headaches. But now everything's back to normal and so I'll go ahead with my letter.

In the meantime you had a birthday, and I hope you had a joyous time and were loved and spoiled. I'll be thinking of you even more than usual on the 24th. Did you receive the books? I sent you my Schiller; why should I buy one as long as I had this one, and I hope that you will enjoy the other two books as well. Write me about it all, in detail.

I'll try to answer your letter of the 3rd as thoroughly as possible. You will probably have received various letters from me in the meantime; please let me know which letters you've received. For instance, did you get the letter in which I wrote about Mr. Landau? In any case, whether my letters reach you or not, be assured that I am *constantly* thinking of you, that I always empathize with you, and that I live my life in you, as you in me. And you must be as sure of me as I am of you. And even if oceans were to come between us, *nothing,* absolutely nothing, could change that.

It's true that we haven't seen each other for a long, long time, but I hope the time will soon come when we can talk about everything in detail. First we will look at each other

inquiringly, but then we'll understand each other as thoroughly as we always have. You must never think that you are alone,
and even if there's nobody there for you, you will always have
me, and I will try to help you and to advise you as best I can
and in any way I can.

When I was your age—and, to be honest, until quite recently—I was often in the same sort of mood you were in on the
3rd. At the moment I don't sink into these moods because I
have someone who wants to and does understand me completely. And someday there will be someone for you, too,
besides myself, whom you will be able to trust completely.
But my dear Kitten, wait patiently, and think long and carefully before you trust another person. On the one hand, I'm
sorry that you have already experienced disappointments, but
on the other hand, it will teach you to be more careful. We,
you and I, seem to have the same disposition: we both want to
trust and believe in other people because we ourselves are so
open and straightforward. As a result, we are happier, but we
also suffer more disappointments. Marion is different in this
respect. She has no need to open up to other people. This is
not a value judgment, neither of her nor of us. I wrote to her
that she ought to be inwardly more modest; I hope it helps. I
feel so powerless, and that often makes me sad. I'm convinced
that if we could talk, we would come to an understanding, and
that you would no longer be sad. After all, you are essentially
a cheerful person and ought be happy and radiant.

Have faith in yourself! We can accomplish much more than
we think. Once, when I was only a few years older than you, I
said to an older woman whom I respected very much (Dr.
Loewenberg): "I'd like to have a very hard life so that I can
show what I can accomplish." And that is indeed what has
happened, Kitten. Again and again I managed to do what I had
to do, and there will probably be many more things for me to
do. That's life. Anyone who despairs every time there's a
problem and throws in the towel doesn't deserve all the beauty and the splendor this world has to offer. Light and shad-
ow—but let's hope no boring gray. And after all, you're a real
trouper, my big brave daughter. Don't wait to hear what oth-

ers are going to say. You must say to yourself, I'll do it this way, and this is the way it is. And you, you little dumbbell, you're not dumb at all; you only have to have faith in yourself. Dear Kitten, I know you so well, and I want to hold you tight in my arms, give you a kiss, and say to you, "Be daring; and whatever you tackle will be interesting."

You know, I really don't like your hairdo in the last photograph I have of you. Was it messed up, or is it because it wasn't parted?

My next letter will go to Marion; perhaps I'll have a chance to write tomorrow, but tomorrow I want to register for a course in "hat making." Can you imagine your Mutti as a milliner? Shall we open a fashion salon together someday? Well, I'm going to start learning how to do those things now.

Many kisses,

Your Mutti

Berlin, February 6, 1941

My dearest Ingelein,

Here's a quick letter for you, too; I'm glad to have this chance to write. Yesterday I had a sweet letter with an enclosure from Susi. Many thanks. She wrote that you had a nice celebration on your birthday. Did Vati happen to be there on January 24? Well now, I'll soon get your version, too, but if you have enough pocket money, please send your letter the same way [special delivery]. (I got this information from Marion, too.) Did you get both of my letters? Georg wrote to me yesterday, complaining that he hasn't heard from you. Have you written him in the meantime? Please do. I sent Gerd a little notebook for New Year's (there's nothing else available here), but he hasn't answered yet. I intend to send him some cigarettes in the next couple of days.

I'm all right, so far. I just got over a cold. And I have a lot of work to do. Making hats is fun, even though I'm just a begin-

ner. I have learned to sew felt and to make a lining. Today I
start my first felt hat. There are fifteen ladies working together; each one, of course, works on something different, and you
can probably imagine what a lot of jabbering there is, with
constant running back and forth. One woman is making a
straw hat, another is blocking her hat, another steams, still
another is trying a hat on, and so on. Wouldn't you enjoy
doing this, too? And Sunday morning we all have to shovel
snow; that's fun, too. It's nice and warm in the apartment, but
in school it's cold, making it impossible to teach for more than
two hours.

[*February 7, 1941*]

Someone came to visit me yesterday, and so I will continue
this today. In the meantime, I received your letter of the 27th.
I'm glad your birthday went so well. Tell me, do other children go to visit their parents in Germany? I miss you so terribly, and we should try to get together soon, very soon. I'm
leaving no stone unturned to accomplish that. I'm confused
about Vati's present. Did he give you a bracelet that will one
day belong to you and Marion, or did he and Marion give you
the bracelet?

Oh dear, I'm always ravenous for chocolate! And it tasted
so good?! Oh well, enjoy it! In the millinery course yesterday,
I reblocked my *old* green hat into a completely new shape; it's
really fun. There's no school today because we can't get the
temperature to go above 5° C [46° F]. Our classroom is right
next to the garden, which is nice in the summer, but now it's
intolerable and impossible to heat.

You're right about Georg; he is jealous. But write to him
anyway. After all, he doesn't know Gerd; so how can he complain about him? Yes, indeed—such things happen. Georg
didn't impress me as being a narrow-minded, petty person;
he's too young for that. But I probably impressed him as too
soignée—do you know what that means?

Yesterday I received a card from Marion, dated January 25,
and her letter of February 3 (it took only three days); pretty

wonderful, isn't it? I'm going to send her a special-delivery letter in the next few days. Timely news is much nicer.

So, please write soon and in detail. Warm hugs and kisses.

Your loving Mutti

Berlin, March 11, 1941

My dearest child,

I received your postcard of the 24th and your letter (via Georg), and I am very happy that you are well and working hard. We are going through troubled times here so that, in spite of my great longing for you, I am glad you are spared this and can work in peace. I wrote to Marion yesterday that many teachers have been fired: of 230 teachers, only 100 remain, and since quite a few of them are tenured (that is, they have been with the [Jewish] Community since before 1928) and cannot be dismissed, you can imagine how bleak my prospects are. A decision is expected by April 1. Messrs. Marcus, Birnbaum, Misch, and Neufeld have already been let go, and now they are assigned [by the Community] to finding apartments for young people who don't have any.

And all these worries and many others have robbed me of the peace of mind required for reading. When I do read, then it's the old things: Goethe, Schopenhauer, Nietzsche—I only have to read a little to get a lot out of it, or I'll read a suspenseful novel that distracts me from my troubles. I just read *Rebecca,* an excellent book with an interesting plot that also contains some very good psychological studies.

Most days I'm in bed by 9:30. How was the concert on March 5? Who sang the Wolf songs? Was the concert in Nyon? Our concert on the 1st was so marvelous that it made me forget all my troubles—except that I thought even more intensely of you. I'm going to wait just a bit, till the sun revitalizes me a little, before I have some photographs taken, and then I'll request permission to send them to you.

I haven't talked with Vati since he returned from Gland. Georg wrote that you might go to Italy; oh, how I would like to join you. Do you know any more about these plans? I can't understand why you don't show your letters to each other— I'll mention this to Marion. too—because even though I write quite different things to each of you, there are no secrets. And if there is something that the other doesn't have to know about, then you can keep *that particular* letter to yourself. But in general, this isn't necessary. I believe you when you say you are trying hard to be kind to Marion, but be patient. She's becoming more sensible with every passing day.

Mrs. Goldschmidt is no longer living in her beautiful apartment but has moved to a boardinghouse. She hopes to be able to leave for Cuba on April 6 and from there to go to her children in the United States. Do you have Uncle Paul's address? Did you ever hear from Uncle Hans Zucker?

What is Georg planning to do? I do not understand how one can have such a listless attitude; or did something else keep him from taking his graduation exam?

And now, my dearest, keep loving me as much I love you. I hug you and kiss you and hold you close—oh, if only I could!!

Your Mutti

Berlin, March 17, 1941

My dearest Inge,

I received your letter of March 6, and I'm surprised at you. You're surrounded by the most beautiful natural landscape, living in refined and loving surroundings, you have no cares, and still you're so irritable and nervous. In my last letter to you I wrote how happy I am, in spite of my great longing for you, that you are growing up there, far away from our terrible unrest and hectic lives. After all, it's your obligation to look wonderful and to be lively and cheerful. The only explanation I can find for your mood is that it's spring. Often one feels depressed in springtime—it happens to me, too—but these moods pass quickly. Spend a lot of time outdoors; watch the plants develop and grow and be glad that after the apparent death of winter, everything begins anew.

You complain that I write so rarely: First. That's not true, Kitten. I write to both of you, and I wouldn't mind at all if you were to show your letters to each other. Also, I have to chide you for not reacting to my letters. For instance, I wrote you two long, detailed letters for your birthday, which you apparently were happy to receive, but that was the only reaction you had. Please read these letters again and pay more attention to everything in them. While I write, I have your letter lying next to mine, and I reply as much as I can to everything you ask about or touch on. Please do that [with my letters too], otherwise we're writing past each other instead of to each other.

Then you're surprised that I occupy myself only with school, English classes, and making hats. Dear Ingelein, you've probably forgotten what things are like here! None of these activities are games we're playing, and it takes up all my time. You know as well as I do that I cannot stay in Germany. I can't and I won't go into details, but I must try to get to another part of the world (maybe there is some way out, but not Paraguay); perhaps I can emigrate to the United States. But I will have to work there to support myself and to earn enough so I can send for you. What subjects would I teach in America? I have little hope for a livelihood as a teacher there. And for that reason I'm learning the millinery trade. Hats are worn everywhere. (Did you think I'm doing this just to make a little hat for myself?) Oh, no, if I can't earn a living as a teacher or by cooking and doing housework, then perhaps I can do it with hat making. Whatever you know you know, and such skills are the only assets no one can take away from you.

And now I'd like to discuss your worries about a career; I can't stop thinking about that, either. I think it would be good if you were to take the interpreter exam, but in my opinion you have to have your Abitur for that. Find out exactly what the requirements are. Nobody is equally talented in all areas, and there will always be something that will be harder to learn or to achieve than another subject. This is how you prove your strength of character: by accomplishing something even though it is difficult. After all, you don't have to get a 1 [the highest grade] in every subject. But you can certainly get a "satisfactory" in every subject. I found math and chemistry very difficult; physics was easier, and with a little help from my teacher, who also taught biology, in which I was good, I passed the exam. Always try and try again, and again, because this is the serious side of life. After all, you want to make something of yourself someday, to be able to earn money so that we can be reunited. Kitten, study, work, make good use of your time. It would be great if you improved in the home economics course with Miss Mettler. Well, as I said, first graduate, and then the world will be your oyster. Can you find out whether the Abitur you take in Switzerland is also valid in the U.S.A.? I would be interested to know. Please answer this letter in detail.

Beneckes came to see me yesterday, but without Renate, who is now entering the seventh year of Obersekunda [secondary school]. At present she isn't the best of students, but that doesn't matter. She likes to dance a lot and often, and on Sunday there is to be a Purim party in school at which she will play the piano. All the students passed their Abitur, including Judith Heimann from the Lessler School (her grade was "good").

I see a lot of Alfred (Fredy) Friedländer's parents. His mother is in the hat-making class with me. Miss Anker is stuck in Lisbon. She did not take the ship on which she was supposed to sail for Cuba.

I've been seeing the dentist for weeks. My schedule for today reads: 9:30–10:00, dentist; 10:15–1:00, hat making; then I go to eat somewhere; 3:00–5:00, school; 6:00–7:30, English. Would you believe me when I say that I'm tired when I get home?

How are you getting along with Marion?

And now, best wishes and kisses

With much, much love,

Your Mutti

Berlin, April 8, 1941

My dearest Ingelein,

I was expecting a phone call from Georg while I was writing a letter to Marion, but it didn't come through. However, I have just spoken with him, and I invited him over for tomorrow (Wednesday evening). I'll surely get to hear all kinds of things then, and I'm really looking forward to it. Perhaps Vati will call, too; that would be very nice.

I haven't heard from you in a long time. G. said on the phone that you had written to me, but I haven't received those letters yet. In the meantime, did you get my letter and the book I sent? Actually I wanted to send you *Wilhelm Meister,* but shortly after Easter you'll be getting my entire set of Goethe (ten volumes)—that is to say, these books are for you and Marion.

How are you feeling these days? A little bit better? At Easter time there'll surely be new students, and perhaps there'll be one among them whom you'll like?! How about your career worries? Please write me all about it. Can you cook a little by now? That would be wonderful. How is the food there?

I am all right, so far. The final decision about whether I am to remain at the school has been postponed to May 1; I hope they will keep me on, but this uncertainty, as you can imagine, is dreadfully hard on the nerves. I already wrote to Marion (unfortunately, I couldn't get a postal reply coupon for her) that we aren't getting any vacation. We have to work for the Housing Advisory Service of the [Jewish] Community. Still, we'll probably get the holidays off. We just found out that for the time being there will be no matzos, and Friday is Passover eve; that's too bad.

Mrs. Goldschmidt (Hella and Edgar's grandmother) is still here, but she hopes to be able to leave after Easter. However, she had to get out of her apartment and has moved into a small room (about half the size of ours). I hope you'll get more Easter eggs than I will be getting and that you'll have a pleasant time. You can probably sit outside in the garden already; here it is still bitterly cold.

Well now, my dearest, all the best and many kisses and hugs. I miss you very much.

Your Mutti

Berlin, June 1, 1941

My dearest Inge,

Perhaps you are upset because I haven't written in such a long time, but even with the best of intentions—I meant to write every day—I didn't get to it, and in the evenings I was simply too tired. Work at school is very strenuous now. Because of the dismissal of so many teachers, we work longer hours while at the same time our salaries have been cut. But the [Jewish] Community is not doing well [financially], and there's nothing that can be done about it. The many hours of teaching physical education (twenty-four hours a week) are very tiring, but I have today off, and so I can have a good chat with you. It's too bad that you already had the Schubert lieder, but don't send them back because they won't exchange them here after all this time and in view of their long journey. When I get the chance, I'll send you easier songs; I'll also be sending you the Goethe volumes in the near future. It's possible that I'll be speaking with Vati tomorrow, and I will try my best to arrange for us to be together during the summer vacation. Are any of the other children in your school going to Germany? Please let me know immediately and give me their names. Perhaps I can join forces with their parents.

Didn't you promise me a photograph of yourself? Naturally it would be ever so much nicer if I could see you actually standing before me, if we could talk to each other face to face!

Are you working hard in school? You can do just about anything if you put your mind to it, and even though you'll never get to be a genius in math and chemistry, we'll all be pleased if you get a grade of "satisfactory."

Have you had good news from Gerd? And when is Uli coming? Our vacation has been severely shortened, but that isn't the final word, either. Now they're saying from July 13 to August 4—three weeks.

Today we are having the most wonderful summer day: it's warm and there's a light breeze blowing. Later I hope to go for a walk in the Grunewald. How lovely it used to be: to have one of you on my right, the other on my left—oh, if that could only happen again. One no longer sees any girls from the Lessler School; they're all gone. Do you still hear from anyone, former classmates or teachers?

You ask whether I play the piano. No, Kitten, not any more. I don't feel like it at all, but I hope that you'll soon be able to play something for me. How is the new teacher?

I have heard nothing more from G.; I hope you haven't, either, and I trust the matter is closed for all of us. Do you spend much time with Brigitte? I still owe her a letter and will write her soon. And how are you now getting along with Marion?

What are you reading? Can you go swimming already, or is the water still too cold?

Please write me often, a lot, and in detail. I wish I could hold you in my arms; I long for you.

Your
Mutti

Berlin, June 9, 1941

Dearest children,

Well, Marion dear, didn't I fulfill your wish promptly?

Just by coincidence I was in town that day and that is how it happened. Your Goethe will be on its way, dear Inge—the books are being shipped on Friday. Have you been enjoying the beautiful weather? Did you go swimming? I am sitting on the balcony right now; the sedum is growing rampantly and protects me from the eyes of strangers. Tomorrow I'm going to Pichelsberg on an excursion with the senior class. The girls are fourteen years old and I'm on very good terms with them, because when I'm with them, I always think of you and so I'm very nice to them. We're taking along a large ball hoping to play "Ball über die Schnur" and Völkerball, etc. in the woods.

Last week I saw Vati. He thinks it would not be good for us to meet during the vacation—unfortunately, I have to concede that he is right. Hard as it may be, we have to resign ourselves to this for the moment, but I still hope that we will see each other soon. Nor will Vati be coming to see you in the near future; he is very busy. These are extraordinary times, and we must all submit to the inevitable. The important thing is that you are all right.

Let me know if you need anything. I'm happy whenever I hear that you're being well cared for. Enjoy this marvelous time; things will never again be as lovely and carefree. You'll realize this only after it's past. I think the school insignia idea is a fine one; but I'm curious whether you'll ever get your awards.

Are many of the students staying in Gland throughout the vacation; are you expecting visitors again?

I feel fairly well. I'm happy when nothing unusual happens, because it's seldom good. Aunt Irma is working in a factory. She likes it there, even though she doesn't earn much money; still, she and her mother have to be able to live on it. Last week she was off on vacation in Hasserode in the Harz Mountains. She didn't gain any weight there; there wasn't much to eat, but she looks suntanned and refreshed. They got an affidavit from America and hope to be able to emigrate in about half a year. I spoke with Goldsteins there [sic]; their daughter (you know her) is in Palestine. But they have not heard from her.

Aunt Margot wrote via Geneva that she is doing all right. She works as an orthopedist in a hospital. Little Eva, she says, writes English so well that her teacher has advised her to make use of her literary talent to become a professional writer.

Now we've chatted a little, and I look forward to your detailed letters.

Affectionate kisses and many loving hugs

Your loving
Mutti

Berlin, September 7, 1941

My dearest child,

You've probably been anxiously waiting for a letter from me. Has Harald come back in the meantime? If so, he probably told you about me, that I'm doing relatively well. And he told me such nice things about you; it made me quite happy. But isn't it funny that a stranger should know more about my children than I do. I had hoped to get a letter from him by now, because he promised that he would report on his conversation with Vati. If everything can be arranged, and I hope it can, for your education and vocational training, it will prove to be a fruitful as well as a pleasant time for you, and you will be well prepared for life. You'll be able to make something of it with skill and hard work. It's a trade needed all over the world. Naturally, after that, it will be up to you whether you'll become a little seamstress or a great artist. But I have faith in you. In addition, there's no harm in learning typing and stenography. No one can take from you the things you know how to do. Yes, of course you can write to me on the typewriter. And please, write about other such pleasant things. I was so happy that you two sisters have finally found each other. What's your new teacher like? Harald was quite enthusiastic about him.

Well, now to get to your letter of the 30th. I'm glad that Vati took it the right way. I was really worried that he would react angrily — which would have been entirely possible. You were lucky. It would be nice if you and Marion had long and detailed conversations with each other about books, etc. I think she is reading books that are much too difficult for her. What are you reading right now? Have you heard from Gerd? Where is he? When is Karin Grelling arriving [here]? Of course I will look after her. Tell her to call (86 63 92). Is she part-Jewish? What professional plans does she have? Perhaps I can smooth the way for her a little. I am always glad to have direct news about you. When Harald or Miss Mettler tells me [about you], it's of course quite different from hearing a schoolmate's version. That's as it should be.

I have to go to school now. Last night we slept very little,
and school starts at 10 o'clock, and the children are very restless. Please write soon and include a lot of details. Many affectionate kisses, embraces, and cuddling.

Your loving
Mutti

Berlin, September 26, 1941

Dearest Inge,

You know, you're really a lazy letter writer. I haven't heard
from you since the 10th, and I'm sure you have many things to
tell me. What did Harald accomplish in Geneva? Will you be
attending the dressmaking school there? And how is your life
shaping up? Where did Brigitte go? I can easily imagine that
you will miss her. I hope you will soon find someone with
whom you can become friends.

Marion wrote that you and she now know that Vati has
remarried. He didn't want me to write to you about this
because he wanted to tell you himself. But now it will be difficult for him to visit you. It was a big surprise for me, too. He
told me half an hour before he introduced me to his new wife.
But it's all right this way—as far as I can judge, she is a splendid woman, who more than anything wants what is best for
you. She is familiar with Vati's business and can continue to
work [there]; otherwise you would have had to come back.
Yesterday, in a letter to Marion, I suggested that she write to
her, perhaps along these lines: Dear Mrs. Asmus, We found out
from Mutti today that you are the one who is making it possible for us to stay here, and we thank you very much. We hope
that the war will soon be over so that things will be easier for
you and Vati. With warm regards, Yours, Inge and Marion.

I think it would be good to do that. What do you think?
She looks pretty and elegant, a little taller than I am, very slim,
dark. Before this her name was Mrs. Neiner; her husband was
Jewish. She divorced him.

I like your sweater very much. I have one that is quite similar in brown and green. It has a brown pocket at the top on the green side, and on the brown side a green pocket at the bottom. Perhaps that would look nice on yours, too. Oh, if only I could see you wearing it, then I would put mine on, too.

Marion wrote that one of your fellow students would come to see me—I look forward to that, but so far I haven't heard from him. I would have time [for him] next week because we have a lot of time off—but I won't fast [on Yom Kippur].

Aunt Irma has just come in, and she sends you best regards.

Well—now please sit down and write me a detailed letter about what you think and feel.

Many loving hugs and kisses.

Your loving
Mutti

Berlin, October 16, 1941

My dearest children,

Don't be mad at me for writing to both of you in the same letter. At the moment it's really easier for me this way, and since I know that you are now getting along so well together, it is certainly the right thing to do.

First, about me. We have serious worries and are living through a very grave time. I can't and won't burden you with details; I'm fortunate in being better off than many others. You don't have to worry about me. Because of my special status I hope to be able to go on living here as before. Should there be any change, I would notify you immediately, but I don't think there will be. In any case, I join you in hoping that peace will come very soon, and that we will again be able to see and talk to one another. Oh, if only I could take you in my arms and hold you close! Or you could take me in your arms! Because now I'd probably be the littlest of us three. But then I'd put on shoes with very high heels.

And now about you. I haven't heard from Günti yet, and

I'm so anxious to see him. If you don't want me to, I won't give him your letter, dear Marion, but I don't find him that "shallow" at all. However, your wish is my command. My next letter will be your birthday letter. And how do you like sewing, my sweet Inge? Learn a lot, learn everything you can—then you can decide what you have the most flair for. For the time being you don't need to make a final decision. I'm eagerly looking forward to seeing your next letter. Please tell Harald that I'm anxiously awaiting the photocopies—they could turn out to be very important for me.

Your description of the new teaching staff was very interesting; Harald had told me that he was glad to have found such splendid people.

I have had ten different photographs taken of myself; you'll get one of these very soon. Dearest Inge, you were going to send me a photo; and what about you, Little Macaroon-with-braids?

I am glad Brigitte found a good job. What does she say in her letters? And Gerd? Did you get another nice, detailed letter? Where in the world is Günti?

Marion dearest, your views on people and the purpose of life are quite correct, and applicable to most people. But one also has to be somewhat careful, because often your friends might get the idea that you feel more for them than you actually do, and that could have quite unpleasant consequences. Years ago, this happened to me! I was talking to a man who meant nothing to me; suddenly he told me he loved me, and I was horrified. Then he said (he was French): "Even though your lips may say one thing, your eyes tell me that you love me!" But that wasn't true at all. Anyway—Be careful, ladies—this is a serious danger for all three of us. Isn't that true, dear Inge? What's your opinion?

Well, now I'm going to bed. Good night, my beloved children—I feel very close to you, and I know that you'll keep faith with me.

Affectionate kisses and many hugs.

Your Mutti

Berlin, October 23, 1941

My dearest child,

Why do you write so seldom? In these hard times, your letters are more important to me than bread. I am terribly sorry that I couldn't send a happier letter to Marion for her birthday, but I feel so very sad — not at all like the person you used to know — and at the moment I can't imagine a time when things will ever be all right again. You two are my only hope; I am waiting for you. Otherwise, I would have taken another way out. And for that reason you must write often. Only two weeks ago I still looked as cheerful as I do in this photograph — and now?

Did you celebrate a little? How was the birthday? Write me about everything. Did you hear from Vati? I haven't, since Pentecost, and he hasn't sent me his address, but there are probably reasons for that.

How do you like sewing? What are you making? What is your class schedule like? Write me about everything, my dear child. Was Marion pleased with the music book and the sheet music? Did you give her a gift, too? Up to now I haven't heard from your friend Günti. Is he actually in Germany?

Warmest wishes and kisses and many, many hugs.

Your loving
Mutti

How is Marion's hand? She ought to be very careful and write only personal news, nothing of a general nature.

Berlin, November 2, 1941

My dearest children,

I am writing in a somewhat better mood today because a miracle has happened. Heinz L. was gone and has come back. I'll tell you the rest some other time. But there is one thing I want you to know. I would have gone with him, even if it meant misery and hardship and death, but I did not want to nor could I desert you. I see it as my loving duty to preserve a home, a refuge, and myself for you. It was difficult to let this man go, but I am your "mother" first, and only then a "woman." Do you see what I mean? But I also know that my loyalty to you (and with this I have proved how deep it is) is reciprocated by you, and that you will feel this loyalty to me always.

I am very sorry that I wasn't able to speak to Harald; I saw him from the train, but I couldn't reach him anymore. There was much, very much I would have wanted to tell him. Ask him to explain. As soon as I'm somewhat more composed, I will write him a condolence note.

Susi is coming to visit me tomorrow.

Do you understand why Vati is not trying to help me in this desperate situation? Don't write anything about this, but form an opinion about [his behavior].

With great love, I place my trust in you.

Your Mother

Berlin, November 5, 1941

My dearest Inge,

Well, today I can reciprocate and type my letter to you because one of my colleagues has left her typewriter here for an extended period of time.

What do you think of my photographs? Have I changed a lot?

At the moment I feel somewhat better because I'm not alone. Both of us [Heinz and I] still think it was a miracle. We don't know how long this miracle will last, but long ago we rid ourselves of the habit of thinking beyond the next day. I won't be hearing anything from Uncle Alfred in Cologne for a long time; for the time being, you needn't write to him.

The day before yesterday, Susi came by for a visit. She is really a nice girl, and we talked the whole time about you.

When she walked into the room, she said: "This is my past," because she felt that she had been in my room often before, since she knew everything in detail, through both your descriptions, and especially through yours, dear Inge. Aunt Irma also stopped by just then and enjoyed the refreshing, not-at-all-stupid manner of this young person. In these times, it does one good to have such lighthearted people around. She is really a part of you, and I'll invite her again soon. She hopes to take her Abitur in the fall, even though she is really too young. Inge, dear, she advises that you try to do it, too, but she'll probably write you about all this herself. In any case, I was very happy to have her here.

Big changes in the school, too, and it's really a wonder that I'm still there. Another fifteen women teachers were dismissed because the number of pupils has decreased markedly. On December 1, nineteen more will be let go. I'm sure to be among them, but that doesn't upset me so much anymore. When the time comes, I'll do whatever work they assign me to, and I'll be glad if I can earn what I need to live on, and happy to still have a bed and a warm room.

How are things where you are? Is it nice and warm? Please write me in detail just what you are learning in dressmaking school. Do you have nice teachers there, and what are the other students like?

As soon as you get this letter, please go to Harald and ask him to make a photocopy of Marion's juvenile identity card. I forgot to ask him to do this in the letter I sent him, but it may be very important for me.

I sent a condolence note to Georg. He had sent me an announcement of the death of his mother. Have you heard anything from Gerd? How is he? And where are the new pictures of you and Marion?

Well, now you've had mail from me almost every day, and so you'll also have to get busy and write to me. I received a very lovely letter from Marion yesterday; she'll be getting an answer soon.

With affectionate kisses and hugs,

Your loving
Mutti

Berlin, November 25, 1941

My dearest Inge,

Even though I promised Marion that I would also send you a long letter soon, I could not keep my promise because when I come home late at night, I fall into bed, dead tired. But today I worked only from 7 o'clock in the morning until 3:30 in the afternoon—so here is the promised letter.

Marion probably told you that I am no longer at the school (please do me a favor and show my letters to each other; I can't possibly write twice about everything that happens). I am sad not to be with my schoolchildren anymore, even more so because they now have a teacher who is over sixty and does not like teaching. I didn't even say good-bye to the children, since I was dismissed on Sunday and my new work began on Monday at 7:00 A.M.

What am I doing now? I work in the [Jewish] Community's Kataster [land registry], that is, I have to check to see whether all the people who are registered there are still in Berlin. Since about 70,000 people are involved, you can imagine that the work is never-ending, and it's very boring. But what can one do? Next week I'll probably be assigned to a different job in the housing office; I'll write you about it then. I earn less money, but it's enough to live on, and that's all that matters.

[November 30, 1941]

A few days have passed, and I couldn't write because I had a lot of work. Meanwhile, you probably received my postcard so that you weren't worried. But I haven't heard from you in a long time. Why?

I'm gradually getting used to this different way of life. Today I had a good rest, and that makes the world look a little rosier.

And how are you? The last letter I received from you was dated the 14th. A lot of work is really better than too little, but I can understand how you feel when a job degenerates into drudgery; I don't like that, either. Still, Kitten, your expertise in a trade is your greatest asset. This is even more important today than in earlier times. And someday the three of us want to be able to support ourselves. You write that you wish you had a thicker skin. Mine has slowly gotten thicker, too. I used to be as sensitive as a mimosa plant, but today I can deal with things pretty well. I'm sure you'll be able to master that, too. It's always very important, in both positive and negative situations, to discover and separate the important from the unimportant. You must always ask yourself, "Is it worth all the effort and trouble?"

I've asked you often to send me your class schedule so that I can get a proper picture of your life there. Marion intends to keep a kind of loose-leaf diary and send it to me regularly. I think that's a very nice idea. Perhaps you can find the time to do this, too; even if on some days it's just a few lines and on others more, it would still make me very happy to be able to participate in your lives this way.

Have you heard from Vati? I haven't, and so I would be glad if you would let me know how he is.

Well, my dear child, please write soon and tell me what you would like in the way of books or music for Christmas, because everything takes longer these days.

Best regards and kisses—oh, if only I could give these to you in person soon . . .

Your loving
Mutti

Did I write you that Gerd sent me a very kind letter? I would like to reply but don't know where to send it.

Berlin, December 20, 1941

My dearest children,
Now you've made up for a lot because you've really written diligently. That makes me very happy. First of all, I want to

wish you happy holidays. I'm sure you'll celebrate nicely and make each other very happy. I am sorry not to be there with you, sorry that I can contribute only so little. I don't know if I'll even get time off, but I'll think of you and that will be my holiday. I already look forward to hearing about everything. Please write in detail.

What did you make for Mrs. Duschenes, Marion; and, Inge, whom are you looking after? I can give very little in the way of presents because I have nothing to give. Heinz Landau's birthday is on Christmas Day, but I still don't know what I could give him that would make him happy. Yesterday I sent you some books and sheet music because otherwise they won't arrive in time. But there is no poetry among this material, Marion. I'll soon have another chance, and then I'll send you poetry. I didn't receive your letter requesting the poetry until today. And the music for Marion was not available. Even so, I hope that I found the right things. It doesn't matter how you divide the books, but please don't argue. *Das einfache Leben* [*The Simple Life*] by Wiechert is out of print, so I sent you my copy. Neither Timmermanns nor Wiechert are available just now, Inge, but maybe they will be in time for your birthday.

Marion, I think it was very wise that you wrote to Mrs. Asmus along those lines. I also sent her a written confirmation; after this, everything should be much easier. What is needed is the will to do it; all three of us have to keep trying, and we must not give up. I don't want you to stay here permanently, but four weeks would be marvelous, and it may even be necessary. I don't know whether Vati will have time off for Christmas. In any case, I wrote him that I absolutely must speak to him then. Inge, please write to him about this, too.

I can imagine that you both have a lot of work, but after the holidays that will let up. I am glad that you heard from Uncle Josef, but I don't know why he hasn't written to me in such a long time. I have no address for him. When you write, please send him my best regards. And let me know what you know. What did Vati's wife say in her letter to you? How funny it sounds for me to write that! Indeed, life is jumbled! You've probably noticed that by now.

I was very pleased about your diary, Marion; I'll write more about that the next time, although my next letter will be for Inge because it's her turn. Still, I was tremendously pleased with the diary and lived through it all vicariously. Is Georg in Gland?

And finally, I want to send you best wishes. Celebrate [the holidays] as pleasantly as possible. Who knows what will happen next year, and joy gives you endless strength. And when you have a quiet moment, think of your Mütterlein who longs for you. I hope that next year we will be able to see and talk to one another—that's my most ardent wish.

Give regards to all those who know me. Warmest and fondest kisses,

Your
Mutti

Berlin, December 29, 1941

My dearest child,

I am a little disappointed that I didn't get any holiday greetings from you. But the mail will surely bring something for me tomorrow.

First of all, all my best wishes for the new year. I hope that what every one of us is wishing for will soon come to pass: peace, that is our most heartfelt wish, so that all those who are far away and who are suffering so much can return home. I have one great desire: that we three shall be reunited. Preferably for all time, but if it can't be any other way, then at least temporarily. I have done and will do everything toward this end, and I believe it's your desire, too, and that you will do whatever you can, whenever the chance arises.

On Christmas Day I was very happy, because Susi came to see me and brought sweets that were, and still are, really superb, but above all she was so kind, saying sweetly: "Inge and Marion send you this through me," that I was profoundly moved. Mr. Landau, who was here just then, thought she was charming and intelligent. He said, "I'd like to have a daughter like that, too." What will he say when he gets to know *you?* Susi is skiing in the Riesengebirge [Giant Mountains] just now, otherwise I would have invited her for Sunday since I asked a few people over and she would probably get along well with them: Beneckes and Renate, Mr. Paeschke, and a family named Uhrland. If only you could also come on Sunday — one's wishes have become so very modest. But the vacation will do Susi good because her Abitur is in March; this is not so simple for her, since she is still quite young and is lacking in some areas; but she'll do better in languages than the others. She received a 1 in music and a 2 in English and French. I told her that it won't be so awful if she doesn't make it because she could try again in half a year. But she doesn't want to hear of that.

How were your holidays? Did you prepare all your surprises in time? And did you get some presents, too? Did my packages arrive in time? Did Vati write to you? He didn't write to me.

I'm going to write to Uncle Erich via airmail; that works. What sort of nonsense did he write? He probably forgot that you're already grown-up girls and not little children anymore.

Did you write to Uncle Josef? I'm sure he would be happy to get a long, detailed letter from you.

I've gotten used to my new work and resigned myself to my fate — if only things don't get worse.

And now, my dear child, we've had another little chat, but sadly only a one-sided one. Please write to me very soon and in detail; in that way our close ties will be strengthened and then I'll know exactly what you think, what you are doing, and how you feel. (By the way, did Gerd write to you, and did you speak with Georg?)

Affectionate good wishes and kisses and many hugs, and from the bottom of my heart, best wishes for the New Year.

Your loving
Mutti

❁

1942

JANUARY 11–DECEMBER 17

Berlin, January 11, 1942

My dearest children,

Today my letter to Inge was returned, and I hope I am right in assuming that the reason for its return is that you were away on a little trip. I'm sending you both letters now, but not by registered mail, because I think it's more certain that they will reach you this way. In the meantime I've received plenty of mail from you, which makes me very glad. It seems that you enjoyed the holidays and that they were also quite profitable for you. Just think, last night I dreamed that I was at a party and that I danced a lot. Oh, if only it were true! That would mean, first of all, that we would be at peace, and we'd all be better off, and our hearts would be happy again.

We are going through a very grave period here. This time Walter Matzdorff and many of my pupils are on the list [for deportation]. I have to work hard and try to help as many people as possible. I just talked to Susi; she is back from her winter vacation. Naturally she turned in her skis, and toward the end it all thawed. But I only found out on January 9 that she had had a birthday. I'll give her a little present, even if it's late. She has to cram like mad now.

In my next letter I'll reply more specifically to your various letters. I want to send this off as quickly as possible so that you won't worry about me. I'm well and able to work; that's already a lot. I'll write more soon.

For today, affectionate and heartfelt kisses,

Your loving
Mutti

Berlin, January 16, 1942

My dearest Ingelein,

Your photographs are on the desk in front of me. The entire left-hand corner of the desktop is filled with them, and just now it seemed as if you were entering the room, though, mind you, through the door from the balcony—and I gave you a firm birthday kiss. I actually felt us embrace and kiss. And now we are sitting on the couch. Marion is of course here, too, and I put my arm around you—we can move the pillow aside—and we speak to each other with love and warmth. What do I wish for you? That these hard times will soon be replaced by a better time; that peace will come soon and we can be together again, healthy in body and soul. And you must do everything to fortify yourself, inside and out, because much will be expected of us, not just now but also later on. You are very fortunate to have the opportunity to study a lot and to have the time to educate yourself so you can become a really well-rounded person.

Take Gisela Michaelis, for instance; she is one of Aunt Irma's coworkers now and has to leave the house at 5:00 A.M.; she has to do the same dull, tedious work all day long. And when she comes home in the evening, she is content to simply go to bed. You're much, much better off. You can study, you're surrounded by refined, educated people whom you don't immediately have to categorize, and you live in this glorious natural setting. Make use of this time, my dear child, and enjoy it!!! Oh, if only I could be there with you. You won't believe how much I long for you. But we must be sensible.

I read the letter from Leipzig. I'm sure Mrs. Asmus's intentions are good, even though she can't quite conceive what our separation means to us. For the time being, we must be content and hope that Vati isn't having too difficult a time. But it is extremely cold in the East, and there will be many hardships for him there. We are again going through a difficult time here. Actually some of my acquaintances are among those [to be deported], but not my closest friends, and I am deeply grateful for that.

I am sure that I could not arrange a birthday celebration for you here as lovely as the one you can have there. There's only one thing we want to hope and wish for: that there will be peace very soon, and that all of us—Vati, you two, and also I—will live to see it in good health and without inner damage, and that we three will again be able to live together. That must be our goal!!

And now, my beloved big daughter—seventeen years old—a glorious age! No longer a child and yet not old enough to have heavy obligations. All ages have their pluses and minuses, but seventeen has only pluses, for one is already aware of what "life" means. Enjoy yourself and be happy. And when you turn eighteen or, I hope, even sooner, then we will celebrate together!!! And perhaps Gerd can be there too; let's hope and wait for it patiently.

Dearest child, my heart and my thoughts are with you and Marion, always and always.

I hope the books will get there in time (the second copies of the calendar and Wiechert—of which I sent two—are for Marion). Some of the things in the Christmas package were unfortunately returned to me—I was already beginning to wonder what had happened to it; in the package was *my Einfaches Leben,* that is to say, my own copy).

Let them spoil you, let them love you, let them celebrate you, but remember that *here* there is a mother's heart that loves you the most, always.

Your Mutti

Berlin, March 18, 1942

My dearest children,

It's been a long time since you got a detailed letter from me, but I really couldn't write. Now I am well again; you mustn't worry about me; I'm also back at the office, and since we have a lot of work, I use these precious morning hours—the clock is just striking 5:00—to chat with you.

It just occurred to me, Ingelein, that you haven't thanked the Marcus family for the congratulations they sent for your birthday. That isn't right. Mr. Marcus is having a difficult time. He works in a factory as a laborer; this week his hours are from 6:00 in the evening to 6:00 in the morning (when I take the bus into the city, he is just coming home), and last week he had to get up at 4:00 in the morning to go to work. His wife helps him valiantly and tries to make things as easy for him as she possibly can.

Now, to your letters. By now, dear Inge, you've probably received the book for Miss M. I hope I chose well. I gave away the children's book a long time ago; besides, I couldn't have sent it for another reason. It's been some time since I last spoke with Susi, because I don't want to disturb her while she is working. I'm very glad that you are now content, and I'm sure you will feel inwardly more at peace when you see that your work is progressing. You don't need to rush, but I will be tremendously satisfied and happy when you receive your diplomas, and then Vati will also be proud of his big daughter. I know that you won't neglect to further your education and that you will also go on playing the piano.

On Sunday we visited some good friends and there was wonderful music, a trio (piano, violin, cello); from the window, one could look directly into the forest (Onkel Toms Hütte), and I wished nonstop that both of you could have been there, too.[14] Well—perhaps that day will come.

How did you celebrate Harald's birthday? Did the puppet theater turn out well? And what did Marion give him? (The book for Miss M. is of course a present from both of you.)

So—and now you, dear Marion. Your last letter made me sad. What's the matter? Why are you no longer happy there? Is something not right with Mario? Or is Günti bothering you again? It seems to me that it is much too early for you to be learning about the serious side of life, and what jealousy is, and so forth; later on you certainly won't be spared such things, but when you're fourteen years old, you should have entirely different worries. Still, if you're suffering from such things, then feel free to write to me about it. Just don't take everything too seriously, because human nature is such that it can bear and endure almost anything, and usually (but of course not always) there's no permanent damage. Have a talk with Harald and Inge, and please, please, continue to write in your diary. It gives me endless pleasure, and someday you also will enjoy it. So—the fourth installment, please, and with the same honesty and detail—I'm longing to see it.

And now, my beloved children, I'll finish for this morning. Oh, if only I could walk over to your beds now, take you in my arms, and hold you very close and tight!! Shall I snuggle with you for a while? Five minutes with Inge and five minutes with Marion?

I love you and long for you.

Your Mutti

Berlin, April 2, 1942

My dearest children,

I feel quite guilty for not having written for such a long time, but I have to do a great deal of work that is very unpleasant. During the holidays I plan to write you a detailed letter, and I'll answer your questions.

Today I just want to wish you happy holidays and a nice vacation. Enjoy every beautiful minute; go outside and delight in Nature's flowers, the water, and the mountains.

Marion dear, I'll buy you the sheet music, if I can get it here. Inge dear, did you receive the book for Miss Mettler? Please ask Harald whether he got my letter, and send me the answer right away because it is very important to me.

Any news from Vati? And do you write to him? Help me in these difficult times and write to me often and in detail (even if I don't always answer promptly), because your letters and my thoughts of you are the only rays of hope I have.

I can't write any more today, but you should and you must know that I have but one wish, one desire: to see you again as soon as possible. How much more easily I could then answer your questions, which I understand very well.

I love you so very much.

Your Mutti

Berlin, April 5, 1942

My dearest children,

Actually, Inge, this letter ought to be addressed only to you, because I want to answer the question you had in your last letter; but Marion raised the same problem, and so I'll give you both my opinion. And my next letter will also be addressed to both of you because in it I want to try to answer Marion's other question, which also applies to you both.

It's the evening of Easter Monday. I spent the day with Heinz Landau, and we talked about all the things that are on my mind, because we share all our troubles.

Last evening we went walking for half an hour, and on the way home I passed the Russian church. Since it suited my mood—I was under the influence of your letters—I went inside. (Once, we went there together; do you still remember?) A child (ten to twelve years old) was leading the prayers; in the center of the church stood a coffin decorated with flowers, and many people were lighting candles and praying with great devotion. On the way home these thoughts came to me, and that's what I'm now going to write to you:

We all have one God, whether we are Protestant, Catholic, or Jewish, or even if we profess no dogma. When we hear music or enjoy nature, even when we look at the smallest flower, we sense an omnipotence without being able to define exactly where this power resides—it is just there, and we bow before it and believe humbly in it. The oldest religion that recognized this is Judaism, and Christianity built upon its foundation.

Therefore, dear Inge, if as you wrote, you found comfort and peace in reading the Psalms, you probably know that the most beautiful of the Psalms were written by David and other men who lived at that time. And in your religion class you have probably been taught who Jesus was. Marion, you're right in saying that I brought you up so you would become familiar with everything and then make your own choices someday, because I think that the best thing parents can do is to give their children all the information [they need]. Then when they are sufficiently mature and have the knowledge, they must chose on the basis of their inner feelings that which will give them the most in return. You must, however, be aware that one can't change one's faith like a shirt. Rather, when you say, "I am going to profess my faith in the Christian religion," then you have to stick to it.

As far as disloyalty toward me is concerned, dear Marion, that's not an issue here. Nothing will change between us, for our love has nothing to do with this; it is a completely separate matter. I was born a Jew and would never have committed myself to another religion. You two have a choice, and I will not stand in the way of your doing whatever you want to do, so long as your decision is true and genuine and not made just because you are being swayed momentarily. Search your hearts long and hard, and then choose!

I find your question neither naive nor "trivial chatter," for I expect that you are now ready to be taken seriously. I am of course terribly sorry that I can answer your questions only by letter, but let's be grateful that at least this is possible. Whatever happens, however you decide, I will always love you deeply and I will, I hope, always understand you.

Your
Mother

Berlin, May 15, 1942

My dearest children,

I was very happy to get your good wishes; many thanks. Yes, if things would only go according to all those good wishes, I would be doing very well!

Unfortunately, I couldn't send you a detailed answer before

this because someone jammed my finger in a door and I was in a great deal of pain, and even now it's not quite all right. But I don't want you to have to wait any longer for an answer.

My last letter to you was very serious because the situation was, too. At the moment, though, the outlook is a little better. Still, I want to let you know what might happen one day. It is possible that I may write to you—I can't say when—that one or both of you must come here immediately. That is, it might turn out to be absolutely necessary—it has to do with an illness of mine that I discussed with Harald the last time he was here.[15] So, ask him about it and tell him I suggested that he speak with you about it. I also discussed this with Mrs. Asmus, and she knows about it. Vati knows, too, so you wouldn't be doing anything that goes against his wishes. If it becomes *absolutely* necessary for one or both of you to come here, I'll write to you, and Mrs. Asmus, representing Vati, will get in touch with Harald.

Now I'd like to ask you calmly, since for the time being it isn't necessary to do anything, which of you would like to come to stay with me? Tell me quite frankly how you feel. If it's you, Inge, you would have to go to the Lette School. Susi goes there, too, although she takes different subjects. You could learn to become an expert dressmaker, taking courses in sewing, cutting, and fashion, etc. This training lasts two years, and it would be followed by a year of practical on-the-job training in a dressmaking studio.

Marion, you would attend the languages division of the Luisen Oberschule [high school], which has a very good reputation. As happy as I am knowing you are now in beautiful Switzerland, there would also be many good aspects to being reunited with you. I can understand that leaving Gland would be very difficult for you, and I would ask you to do this only in an emergency. But I know that in such a situation you would gladly make the sacrifice for me. Please write and tell me what you think about all this.

And now back to my birthday. Your congratulations were of course the most important thing that happened to me that day, and they arrived in time. I got a lovely silver necklace

from Heinz Landau and gorgeous flowers, which are still in
my room. And when I got to the office, there was a big to-do,
flowers, and a pearl necklace, just what I had wished for. It
looks as though they really had me neatly tied up with neck-
laces this year! And almost all the children in the school sent
birthday wishes, and the Kittels also fired off a long letter—
they wrote about you, too. I think it's nice that you corre-
spond with Gerda. In the afternoon, Irma and her mother and
a few other people came over; it was quite pleasant.

I wonder whether you will be here with me next year.

As yet I'm not at all temperamentally ready to be a digni-
fied grandmother. Usually people think I'm a young woman,
and if I protest, they ask, "Well, how old are your babies?"

Susi came to visit me last week—she always reminds me of
you. I had the piano tuned. Unfortunately, the man didn't do a
good job, and I had to have another piano tuner come by. But
Susi played very well, primarily Bach. Are you practicing
hard, too? Now I can't go on any more.

Warmest regards, kisses, and cuddly hugs—do you still
remember what that's like? I love you so very much.

Your
Mutti

Berlin, June 2, 1942

My dearest children,

The letters I sent you recently contained less news than any
I've written you in all these years. The reason for this is the
great worries I have with which I don't want to burden you.
But now this can no longer be avoided, and you must share in
my difficult life. My illness has gotten much worse—Harald
probably told you all about it—and I can't get along without
you anymore. So you have to come now, and I know that you
will come gladly and that now we can begin sharing our experiences again. Harald must have told you what may happen if

you don't come. Show me what you're made of. Do your best and think carefully before you do anything! You can leave some of your letters and books there; we'll pick them up later on. Do *nothing* without talking to Harald first.

Since you said that you wished to be baptized, I advise you to do it there because you know Pastor Freudenberger so well and he would surely be pleased to do it. Then the documents can be properly filled out there. Discuss all this with Harald. We won't be able to write each other about the details till I've heard from Harald that everything has been arranged.

My heart is too full, but I can't write much; in any case, I noticed that you, dear Marion, have written very little recently, whereas Ingelein has improved her record. Oh well, sometimes one person has more to say, sometimes the other. Dearest Inge, I received your lovely letter. Perhaps you can still take the exam; it would be very important and a good thing to do and would make many things easier for you here. We have a sewing machine here, and I can already see you working hard for us all. The Marcuses would of course move out [when you join me] so that we'll have the apartment to ourselves.

I just reread your last letter, and I'm really pleased with your attitude toward me and other people. I am sure that we will immediately reestablish the close relationship we have always had. And you too, dearest Marion, will soon feel at home here again in spite of the fact that many, many things have changed. I intend to stand by you with all my might, and I know that you in turn will help me. Heinz Landau will be as good a friend and adviser to you as he is to me.

Please write as soon as possible; I am anxiously awaiting your answer!

With deep love and infinite trust in you—I send kisses.

Your Mutti

Berlin, June 18, 1942

My dearest children,

I was astonished when I read your last letter, for it made me realize that you have not been receiving mail from me. That explains everything because Miss Mettler informed me that the letters I sent to you have been kept from you; they felt it was the right thing to do.

Meanwhile, you were probably briefed and now you know the contents of my letters.

The letter and little package I received from Mrs. Rühler were like a ray of hope for me in this sorrowful time. You made me very happy with that; the will and the thought alone are enough; dear Inge, go ahead and wear the pink pajama if it is not too short for you, and think of me. It's just as though I were doing it. She also writes some very kind things about you. I am going to send her an answer right now, because she seems to be a charming woman. She also wrote that you, dear Marion, didn't grow last year. Are you eating properly, or have you reverted to your old ways?

There's nothing new to report about myself. I still have the same job. Unfortunately, the weather is cold most of the time so that we can't yet make use of the balcony. This year I planted tomatoes in the flower boxes; we'll see how the harvest turns out.

My heart is with you; believe me!

Many kisses and hugs,

Your Mutti

Berlin, June 19, 1942

My dearest children,

You're probably surprised that I have to take this route in writing to you, but if I address my letters directly, we'd run the risk that you wouldn't get them, or only after it's too late. But please keep your lips sealed and tell *no one* about it.

Things are very serious here, and there is just *one* way out for me, and that's through you, either one or both of you. Your letter to me, dear Inge, was very well written and well intended, but these are nice words that unfortunately you use too often, something I've been aware of for a long time. Now action is the *only* thing that matters. If you want to see me again, one of you has to come to stay with me, and as soon as possible.

Please urge Harald to get you both a visa, or just for one of you; and you *can* get visas, especially since Vati is a soldier. Harald only has to *want to do it;* because according to my inquiries, I believe it all depends on his willingness to help.

Everything you wrote, Ingelein, is a delusion; if we can't manage to see each other *now,* there is absolutely no hope for later.

Only your action will prove your love!

With deepest love,

Your Mutti

Berlin, July 12, 1942

My dearest children,

I'm unhappy about many things, but more than anything it hurts to hear so rarely from you. True, people have come between us, but in spite of everything, we must not lose touch. Let's talk to one another again, the way we used to. Dear Inge, you'll get a direct reply to your last letter, but I am expecting to get some news this week, and my answer to you will depend on that.

I went to see the Naumanns today and I spoke with the parents and with Ernst; I also talked to Günter Berg and his sister (from Andernach, I think) who were also in Gland. All three of them found it a bit hard to leave Gland, but now they feel fine here. Ernst will certainly make progress in his profession.

Things are going fairly well with me, but we have a lot of problems here. Dr./Miss Meyer is very sad just now and we are, too, because on Wednesday her mother is leaving.

But now, on to something quite different. The tomatoes on the balcony are flourishing. Sixteen fat tomatoes are already hanging from the branches. I hope they won't drop off prematurely.

Are you helping with the harvest? And are you enjoying your vacations? Dear Inge, is your first examination behind you?

Now, sit down right away and write me a detailed letter. It is my one and only great joy, and I hope you will surely do me that favor.

I love you very, very much and I know that you love me, too. Let me feel it. It's more important to me than air or food.

Many kisses,

Your Mutti

Did Mrs. Asmus come to Gland?

Berlin, July 22, 1942

My dearest Inge,

It's been a month since your last letter arrived, and you can probably imagine how unhappy I am about this. We don't want to believe that the time might come when I would not hear from you or you from me, but as long as we still have the chance, let's write to each other as often and in as much detail as possible. At least once a week, all right?

How are you? Did you pass the first examination, and do you have a different schedule now? Please write me all about it. Do they give you vacations in the dressmaking workshop? Did you make friends with any girls in Geneva? I'm interested in everything you tell me. Nothing has changed with me. I have many serious problems. Our circle of friends is steadily getting smaller. Your former teacher Mr. Neufeld died; he committed suicide. In recent weeks he looked so terrible, you would scarcely have recognized him.

Do you know how much I weigh? Not quite 100 pounds. That's pretty nice for one's figure, but unfortunately it shows in the face, too. Oh, if only things would change soon! My longing for you is enormous.

With many kisses and infinite love,

Your Mutti

August 17, 1942

My dearest children,

I am too upset to sleep, even though I don't have to be in the office today until later. And so I'm sitting on the balcony; instead of flowers, beautiful red tomatoes glow in the flower boxes, and if I were hungry I could eat one right off the vine; they taste wonderfully sweet.

Otherwise my life is full of sad things at the moment. My one consolation is to know that you have a nice home and are happy, healthy, and content. Let me share in your lives and write more often; it is so important to me. I can't imagine that there could be a time when your letters will not reach me, and yet that may already be the case. This time I know that we will be reunited! We must keep this goal in sight and not lose courage.

There are people who have much more than we in the way of superficial things: money, etc., but who, in spite of that, are poor because they don't know that a tiny forget-me-not is much, much more beautiful than a large showy flower. I have never had many material possessions, but I know how infinitely rich I am because I have you and your love—and you have my undying mother's love.

Yesterday Ernst Naumann came to see me; naturally we spoke only of you.

Your pictures are darling, Marion; I am going to wait until I get yours, too, Ingelein, before I have them enlarged. So—send them soon. Now, please sit down and write to Uncle Erich and congratulate him on his marriage, and include me, too.

It's 6:00 A.M.; I have to go to the office!
With never-ending deepest love,

Your Mutti

Berlin, August 30, 1942

My dearest Inge,
Today I'll write only to you for a change because your lazy sister has to be punished—I wonder if she's completely forgotten her mother.

Your two letters made me very happy. It's nice to have good friends on whom one can truly rely. Please send me her exact address—I mean Margot's—I want to thank them for being so nice to you two. In any case, please give them my regards.

Now that your work has begun again, I hope it will bring you joy and success. Have you ever worked for other people before? It's much harder than working for oneself; I know that from having made hats. Not every material and not every style suit everyone, and it is a special art to adapt yourself to other people's tastes.

[September 4, 1942]

I have the same problem you do. I start a letter and then it lies around for days. But I had a lot of unpleasant work to do in the meantime, and in this heat it is all twice as hard, and in the evenings I am so worn out that I can't do anything anymore. But I was very happy to receive such nice letters from you and Marion. So I take back what I said at the beginning of this letter.

Enclosed is a letter from Gisela, who just happened to come to our office. She has grown pretty as a picture and lives on her own with a girlfriend. She is seeing a nice young man whom she introduced to us. I'm glad you read Ibsen's *Baumeister Solness* [*The Master Builder*]. Heinz Landau and I once read it aloud, taking the different parts, and we often talked about it; that was in the days when our minds were still somewhat serene. I always had such ambitious plans, and often I had a mistaken impression of people because I saw or wanted to see only the good in everybody. Then, when you look at your ideal with sober eyes and realize that everything isn't what it seemed to be, it's hard.

Which leads me to your friendship with Gerd. I can't nor do I want to say anything against him, but I think that you two don't know each other well enough. The day may come, and let's hope it will come soon, when the two of you will get to know each other better. Don't think I don't understand how you feel, or that I'm unhappy that you and Marion will soon be adults. On the contrary—we can now talk to each other more and more as friends, and we can be friends. But you hit the nail on the head when you said that I regret terribly to have to watch you grow up from afar—having missed this time together, one can never make it up later. But the hope that our separation will not last too much longer will and must sustain us.

Miss Schwartze and her mother are no longer here.

For the time being I will stay.

I wish you fun in your work. Many kisses, hugs, and loving thoughts,

Your loving
Mutti

It's not the end of the world that Vati and Mrs. Asmus haven't written to you; they don't write to me, either. And you know Vati; he'll write to you next time, you'll see.

Berlin, September 28, 1942

My dearest Ingelein,

Your lovely letters make me so very happy, now that they

are coming regularly, and you give me reassurance, which is of great value to me these days—more than you can possibly know. Your letters are like sounds from another, a better, world and they allow me to hope that someday we, too, will be able to breathe more easily and calmly.

Today I'd like to take up something you mentioned in one of your recent letters. You wrote that you want to become independent as soon as possible, to earn your own livelihood. I think you're 100 percent correct. By all means, work so that you won't need anyone else [to support you]. From what you write, I'm happy to hear that you find satisfaction in dressmaking; everything one does with love succeeds, most of the time. After you've passed your examination at Christmas time, you certainly won't be perfect yet, and you mustn't allow yourself to get out of practice. I would try to get work in a good dressmaking shop or in a good store. Talk it over with Harald and with your teachers in Geneva, or perhaps with the Enderlins. Housekeeping you can learn on the side; we all did that. And Baruschkes can surely find someone else to help them with the housework.

Who initiated your competition? I think it's a nice idea. Did you have to write something to enter the contest? If so, please send it to me.

I'm fairly well. There are only a few people with whom I still get together, because many have left us, and besides, I have little time and need a tremendous amount of rest in order to keep my spiritual equilibrium. But I hope and believe that the time when we three will be reunited is not too far off, and then I'll be your "little old mother." Still, all this suffering will of course have left its mark on me.

If only we were sitting together again now! If no great miracle occurs, Dr. and Mrs. Opfer will leave this week and will never again hear anything from Margot and little Eva.

Unfortunately, I won't be able to send you the photo album. You'll have to buy your own. Do it, because otherwise you'll lose the little pictures, and that would be a pity. Thanks for the group photo. Ernst had shown it to me before, but in a larger size.

So, my dear child, farewell for today. Many kisses, I love you very, very much. I believe in you and wait for you, and I continue to hope.

Your Mutti

Berlin, October 13, 1942

My dearest Inge,

I have to take advantage of this time while I'm still feeling bright and fresh; so you will both get a letter today. I have your letters of September 16, September 19, and October 5 in front of me. I see that you are really becoming a "mensch" [a real human being], and that makes me very happy. The fact that you derive so much pleasure from dressmaking is a sign that it's the right career for you. It is quite sensible also for you to learn hat making, but don't get the idea that it is simple. After all, you are not learning it the way so-called "young ladies" used to learn all that [in the old days]. You really want to earn a living with it someday—therefore learn it from top to bottom.

Please tell me how you arrived at your plans for after Christmas or Easter. Was there an exchange of letters about that with Vati? I only know what I see in your letters since I have no direct news from Leipzig—I think some people sometimes forget that you have a mother—but I know you do not forget.

You wrote that you went to the circus. Did you know that even as a little child you didn't like going to circuses? You always felt that the animals were being mistreated.

Last week Susi was here, and Ernst and Susi wanted to visit me Friday evening, but something came up at my end, so unfortunately I couldn't see them. Susi is now back in Vienna. Ernst has to work hard because he is preparing for his Abitur in addition to his other job. I wonder if he will pass? This semester, out of twenty-seven students, eighteen failed. That's a very high percentage.

I am really sad to hear that you and Marion do not always get along. With good intentions that ought to be possible, don't you think? Actually, it's true that you complain less often about Marion than she complains about you, but each time it happens, it makes me quite sad. There are so many sad things in this world, and so you ought to be extremely considerate when it comes to the less important things.

[*October 14, 1942*]

My strength was exhausted last night, so I'm finishing this letter in the office this morning.

Please write again soon and make it a long, detailed letter. (I look forward to seeing the pictures; I could have had them enlarged here, too.)

With much love and great longing,

Your Mutti

Berlin, December 6, 1942

My dearest children:

I am firmly convinced that you would behave quite differently toward me if you knew exactly what the situation here is. I am often very sad and depressed; your letters would be the best remedy for lifting my spirits, but I wait in vain. Especially you, dear Marion, are treating me very unkindly. Read the letter from Heinz Landau again and act accordingly. So— now I've scolded you enough.

Dearest Inge, you must surely be working very hard. When is your examination? How long will it be? What do you have to be able to do? Please send me specifics. I'll be crossing my fingers in the hope that all goes well. Have you spoken with

Harald about what you will do after that? Did Vati write to you? You really ought to keep me better informed about what's going on.

Thank God, nothing has changed for me. At the moment— it's Sunday morning—I'm in the office, but I don't have much to do. I ought to be at home cooking, darning socks, etc., but things don't always work out as one might wish.

How was St. Cerque? Can you ski already? Who is your favorite author at the moment? Unfortunately, I have little time to read. I sleep every free minute to preserve my nerves. Can you visualize your mother as a very slim person? How is the food there? Do you still like it as much as before, Inge? And how is your appetite, Marion?

I'm sure your French has improved a good deal from working in the dressmaking shop. Do you still keep up with your English, Ingelein?

Now I have to do some work so I'll close. Oh, if only everything were different! Your chairs here are always empty; will we ever again sit at our table together, having a cozy talk?

Well, let's not lose hope.

Please write to me, write to me!

Many kisses and an affectionate hug.

With much love,

Your Mutti

Did you hear anything from Susi?

Please write to Uncle Paul.

When did you last get a letter from him?

Berlin, December 17, 1942

My dearest Inge,

You probably think that if you write only infrequently, your letters will be more appreciated; oh no, not at all. I am often sad that we so rarely express to each other our determination to stick together (despite the fact that I really believe in it). Should we resolve to write to each other more often in the coming year? I was very happy with your letter of November 29. If anyone understands the longing for giving and receiving, then it is I. But be patient and wait, Kitten. Someday you will find someone who will love you and whom you will love. You don't have to do anything about it; it will happen by itself. And then it is so much more beautiful.

I also received a nice letter and a little package from Georg. He really is a loyal young man and is not at all angry with you.

I'm doing only so-so; if only you were here. I would so much like to be able to laugh again with all my heart; our lives are very serious these days. It is good that I have someone with whom I can share all my burdens, and we don't want to give up hoping that better times are ahead.

Christmas is coming, the celebration of love. Let's hope that peace will come and all people who love one another will be reunited. Sometimes I think that my front door is about to open and you will come storming through, and then I am depressed because it was all just a fantasy. But I am tremendously happy that you are now getting along so well together, and I hope that you will grow even closer over the years.

Marion wrote me a very sad letter. Her friendship with Mario seems to have broken up. Please be her good friend and help her. This evening I'm going to write her a letter, too. It's now 6 o'clock in the morning and I have to go to the office.

So, my beloved Ingelein, have as pleasant a holiday as possible—did you get the books? Please be very kind to each other, and think now and then of me. Much, much love and kisses,

Your
Mutti

✿

Notes

1. At least one aspect of German letter writing in the 1930s
and 1940s is quite different from the current American style.
American salutations and closings are usually brief and for-
mulaic. German closings tend to be more elaborate. In these
letters, however, Hertha Feiner goes beyond even the usual
German form. In these emotional phrases and sentences, I
believe she is trying to convey her love, her longing, and her
concern for her daughters. Therefore, it would be wrong simply to convert them to American style. Yet to translate their
effusive sentimentality literally would make them sound ludi-
crous. I have tried to take a middle road here.

2. *Vati* is a diminutive of *Vater* (Father), used much as
"Dad" or "Daddy" is in English.

3. *Mutti* is a diminutive of *Mutter* (Mother). It is used in
much the same way "Mom," "Mommy," or "Mummy" is in
English, yet it isn't quite the same. Therefore, *Mutti* was kept
throughout, with two exceptions: (1) the one letter Hertha
signed *Mutter,* which was translated to "Mother," and (2) the
one she signed *Mütterlein,* which was retained and means
"Little Mother."

4. "Schnackchen" is how Inge and Marion referred to Miss
Schnackenburg, the Feiners' housekeeper.

5. These were the sisters who founded the Waldschule, also
called Lessler School.

6. Hertha Feiner uses a few affectionate nicknames for her
daughters. *Mariönchen* means "Little Marion." *Makrönchen,*
a playful variation on "Marion," translates into "Little Macaroon." *Muschichen* is equivalent to "Kitten" or "Little Kit-

ten." *Ingelein* means "Little Inge." Usage of *Ingelein* and *Mariönchen* has been retained, but most other nicknames have been translated.

7. A wooded section of Berlin.

8. A certificate that entitled Jews to receive packages from abroad.

9. Hertha is referring to the restrictions being imposed on Jews. She is afraid that she will not be able to write or telephone her daughters.

10. *Oblaten* and *Steckbilder* are little paper seals that were used to seal letters and packages. Youngsters saved and traded them and pasted them into albums.

11. A regional term for "sink."

12. Georg von Prosch was also a student at Les Rayons. His father was with the international Protestant church organization in Switzerland, and Georg was able to go back and forth between Gland and Berlin. Few non-Jews had contact with Jews. But Georg visited Hertha, helping her stay in touch with her daughters. Later this was no longer possible.

13. Abitur is the final set of examinations at the end of secondary school. Passing the Abitur is required for university admission.

14. Onkel Toms Hütte (Uncle Tom's Cabin), a section of Berlin.

15. *Krankheit* means "illness"; the word is used here and elsewhere as a code word for her fear of being deported.

❈

Jewish Lives

HENRYK GRYNBERG
Children of Zion

INGEBORG HECHT
Invisible Walls *and* To Remember Is to Heal

DAN JACOBSON
Heshel's Kingdom

ERICH LEYENS AND LOTTE ANDOR
Years of Estrangement

RUTH LIEPMAN
Maybe Luck Isn't Just Chance

ARNOŠT LUSTIG
Children of the Holocaust
The Unloved (From the Diary of Perla S.)

LIANA MILLU
Smoke over Birkenau

ARMIN SCHMID AND RENATE SCHMID
Lost in a Labyrinth of Red Tape

WIKTORIA ŚLIWOWSKA
The Last Eyewitness: Children of the Holocaust Speak

ISAIAH SPIEGEL
Ghetto Kingdom: Tales of the Łódź Ghetto

ARNON TAMIR
A Journey Back: Injustice and Restitution

JIŘÍ WEIL
Life with a Star
Mendelssohn Is on the Roof

BOGDAN WOJDOWSKI
Bread for the Departed